Lost...
and Found

G P S

When What Happens
Isn't What We Expect

Compiled and Edited by
Yvonne Lehman & Terri Kalfas

GRACE

Royalties for this book are donated to Samaritan's Purse.

LOST... AND FOUND
WHEN WHAT HAPPENS ISN'T WHAT WE EXPECT

ISBN-13: 978-1-60495-093-9

From Samaritan's Purse

We so appreciate your donating royalties from the sale of the books in the *Divine Moments* series to Samaritan's Purse.

What a blessing that you would think of us! Thank you for your willingness to bless others and bring glory to God through your literary talents. Grace and peace to you.

Mission Statement

Samaritan's Purse is a nondenominational evangelical Christian organization providing spiritual and physical aid to hurting people around the world.

Since 1970, Samaritan's Purse has helped victims of war, poverty, natural disasters, disease, and famine with the purpose of sharing God's love through His Son, Jesus Christ.

Go and do likewise.

Luke 10:37

You can learn more by visiting our website at samaritanspurse.org

Dedicated to the many authors

who have so generously contributed their stories

to all of the books in the *Divine Moments* series.

Table of Contents

1

GPS: God's Patient Sovereignty

Ann Tatlock

The night was dark and rain hit the windshield in a steady downpour. Behind the wheel of a rental car, I was in the middle lane of a five-lane interstate highway, surrounded by speeding vehicles on either side. I had no idea where I was or how to get to where I was going, and I was scared to death.

I looked at the GPS sitting mute on the dashboard. "Speak to me, Zelda!" I said aloud, using the nickname I'd given the device at the start of this long trip.

Just as I began to fear that she was broken and I would be forever lost, Zelda spoke, telling me to take the next exit. I did, and in short order I was rewarded with those six sweet words: "You have arrived at your destination."

Clearly, I didn't inherit what my father called his uncanny sense of direction. I've been lost in most of the major cities of the world: London, Paris, Athens, Berlin, Tokyo, Shanghai. You name it, chances are I've wandered around that city slack-jawed, hoping grace would lead me home. Obviously, the fact that I never disappeared altogether means that I was somehow able to get from here to there . . . eventually.

I've found that also to be true in this journey called life. When I was a young teenager, my parents gave me a *Living Bible*. Psalm 139:3 soon became one of my favorite verses: *You chart the path ahead of me, and tell me where to stop and rest. Every moment, you know where I am.* Thankfully, even though I may not have always known where I was, God did! More than that, I felt confident God had a path set for me, that He would help me walk that path in life and that it would take me to exciting places in service to Him.

Being human, though, I have made major mistakes over the years. Some decisions have seemingly knocked me off course, and I've been left struggling with broken relationships and career setbacks. Many days I thought I'd messed up beyond all hope of ever get back on track.

Other times, through no apparent fault of my own, I've ended up in situations I never dreamed of and would have rather avoided. I could only wonder how I managed to get there and whether I would ever get out.

Thankfully, I'm not traveling solo, nor am I my own navigator. God has always assured me that He is with me, guiding my steps. He has charted the path ahead of me, and in His sovereign wisdom, knows exactly where He wants me to go.

When I'm driving and make a wrong turn despite the GPS (yes, I even get lost with a GPS!), I see that little tracking device hurry to recalculate my position and set a new route for me. In the end, I still arrive where I'm supposed to be.

In a sense, God does the same when I make mistakes or when life seemingly knocks me off track. Because He is sovereign, nothing will thwart His plans for my life. He takes the wrong turns and makes them part of the journey while ever working out His purposes for me.

I am so grateful for GPS: God's Patient Sovereignty. I can know I will arrive safely at my destination, because grace is leading me home.

2

Defying Defeat

Pastor James Jones
as told to Diana C. Derringer

For many years Pastor James Jones of Campbellsville, Kentucky, has provided leadership in his local church, community, state and national conventions, and around the world. Yet few know of his challenging beginnings.

"My early life was far from pretty," he has said.

His mother tried to abort him. In no uncertain terms, she let him know he was unwanted. She already had two daughters and believed she was too old for another child. When he was five-and-a-half years old, his parents divorced and she left. Because his father's work often took him out of town, Jones and his two sisters went to a church-sponsored boarding school.

At seven years of age, he contracted diphtheria. Since no one expected him to live through the night, a hospital physician instructed his father to notify his mother.

Again, however, he defied the odds . . . and good came from that health scare. His parents reunited and his mother and one sister became Christians soon after. The other sister trusted Christ a few years later.

But the damage prevailed. Haunted by lingering feelings of

rejection and certain no one loved him, eleven-year-old Jones found acceptance in a gang. In his young mind, joining made much more sense than continuing to receive their regular beatings and theft of his paper-route money.

"Out with the guys one night," he said, "a strange feeling came over me. Certain I needed to get away, I pretended to be sick. Before I made it home, my two buddies, attempting to steal a car, shot the owner and landed in jail. For the longest time when I passed a jail I felt worthless, believing that's where I should have been."

Jones' overwhelming inferiority complex continued until his junior year in high school. When the persistent efforts of one person finally led him to a transforming relationship with God, both his sense of worth and the direction of his life changed.

"God took away those negative feelings," he said.

An added blessing came when his mother finally told him she was proud of him and glad her abortion attempt had failed.

Prior to high school graduation, God called Jones to preach. He began his ministry in college. In addition to serving as a pastor, he led mission teams to several countries. In Russia shortly after the fall of the Soviet Union, his team distributed two thousand Bibles in a single day. Jones said he had never before experienced seeing people with so great a hunger for the Word of God or such a desperate desire for hope. Several of his team members helped construct a church building in Kolpino, Russia.

While in Kenya, Jones found himself at the wrong end of a Maasai warrior's spear. "I'll be honest," he said. "I thought I was a goner!" Yet before the day passed, he had led that warrior and two others to faith in Jesus Christ. That Maasai warrior's spear now hangs in Pastor Jones' study as a reminder of God's marvelous work.

One of his personal friends describes Pastor James Jones as "a healer and reconciler, whose greatest strength is living, preaching, and showing the reconciling power of Jesus Christ." He is noted for the countless thousands he has brought to Christ.

Pastor Jones led his father to Christ about a year or year-and-a-half before his father died. "I can't recall that we ever told each other, 'I love you,'" Jones said. "But I told him [as he lay on his death bed], more than once, even though I wasn't sure he could hear me."

He continued, "People desperately need love. But we can't stop at feeling love; we must tell them we love them, and that God loves them too."

Jones says, "For a poor skinny kid from Birmingham, Alabama, who felt like a zero, a nothing with no ambition, my opportunities have been amazing. By all that is logical, I should never have been born and should have died on at least two other occasions. Yet here I am, still blessed with a wonderful life and serving the Lord the best way I know how."

Pastor James Jones is a beautiful example of the Heavenly Shepherd finding His lost sheep, and making an earthly shepherd of him.

~ 3 ~

Fourth of July Miracle

Lydia E. Harris

The mood was anything but festive when we arrived at my sister's home in Seattle for the annual Fourth of July gathering. Our relatives had just learned that Nicholas, our niece's two-and-a-half-year-old toddler, was missing in the Wyoming mountains, where his family and friends were camping. Little Nicholas had been playing with the other children and wandered away.

Our hearts ached as we fervently prayed for the toddler's safe return. Meanwhile, even though a helicopter searched from the air and more than two hundred volunteers combed eight square miles of Muddy Mountain on foot and by horseback, Nicholas was not found by nightfall.

The next day, a canine team and the Civil Air Patrol joined the search and canvassed the heavily-wooded slopes and sagebrush meadows. After dark, the search coordinator set up twelve listening posts, and a volunteer showed up with an infrared scope. The scope detected wildlife, including scampering mice, and one man at a listening post heard an idling truck three-quarters of a mile away. But no one heard a toddler's cry.

For Nicholas' parents, a pleasant weekend outing had turned into a nightmare mingled with hope and hysteria. His mother told the sheriff, "I see stumps moving and hear squirrels talking." And in her mind, she kept hearing her son cry. She felt so scared that she couldn't bear to join the search.

With no sign of Nicholas for two days, we feared the worst. How could he stay alive in the wilderness without food and water? What wildlife might prey on him? And how could a thirty-month-old child survive alone another night when temperatures dipped? Only God could sustain him . . . and we earnestly prayed He would.

The third day, hundreds of volunteers continued searching the rugged terrain, clambering over slopes and pushing through brush. Many sacrificed their own plans, hoping to rescue a small child.

Fifty-six hours into the search, a motorcycle repairman searched in an isolated area about four hundred yards from the campground. He stopped to pray, walked three steps, and found Nicholas — unharmed! Nicholas was sitting on his clothes in some underbrush, wearing only a diaper. He had made a bed with his clothes in a gully that was almost hidden from view.

"He was scared to death when the searchers found him," his mother said, "but I guess instinct told him that was a safe place to stay."

When Nicholas arrived at the hospital, he was dehydrated but otherwise in stable and satisfactory condition. The police reported that the weather had been warmer than expected those nights.

How we rejoiced and praised God for protecting Nicholas!

Psalm 29 speaks of God's strength, telling us His powerful voice controls even the weather. We believe just as God is sovereign over the thunder and lightning, He spoke in the mountains of Wyoming and the weather warmed.

More than thirty years later, I remember Nicholas's rescue as one of the greatest answers to prayer we have experienced in our family. I thank God for this Fourth of July miracle, when His awesome power far exceeded any spectacular fireworks displays. In His sovereignty and compassion, it seems God changed the weather pattern those two nights and wrapped one small, lost boy in the warmth of His love.

~ 4 ~
With This Ring

Lola Di Giulio De Maci

Mom, Dad, and I hustled into the car and headed west to the big city of Los Angeles. The wedding was scheduled to begin at noon.

When we arrived earlier than expected, Dad pulled into a gas station to clean the windshield and check the tires while Mom and I visited the restroom to freshen up.

A huge, gilded mirror hung over the sink, with a silver-and-white soap dispenser beneath it. Before I washed my hands, I removed my promise ring from my finger and placed it on top of the dispenser. I admired my ring for the hundredth time. It had a lustrous, white pearl in the center of it with six small, sparkling diamonds encircling it. It reminded me that soon I would be the one inviting guests to my wedding.

I shut the restroom door behind me and left.

The church was solemnly quiet. Guests dressed in their Sunday best whispered in muted tones, their words floating heavenward to the buttressed ceiling of the chapel. In this hallowed space, two people would be united in Holy Matrimony.

A deluge of emotions flooded my heart. How would I feel on my wedding day? What kind of gown would I wear? Would

I pick pink roses and white baby's breath for my bouquet? I'd started dreaming of the details the moment I became engaged.

My thoughts were interrupted when the organist began playing *Here Comes the Bride,* Richard Wagner's *Bridal Chorus.* We all stood and faced the bride as she proceeded up the aisle in her white satin gown, her father smiling through tinted glasses.

Soon I would be the bride marching up the aisle on the arm of my father. My father's face had been solemn and wistful when he escorted my sisters to their future husbands. My turn would be no different.

"With this ring I thee wed," the groom professed to his bride, as he slipped the ring on her finger.

My right hand automatically searched for the promise ring on my left hand. There was nothing there! My ring was gone! Gone. I immediately started replaying the morning's events from the time we had left home to this very moment.

Home. Freeway. Gas station. Church.

Gas station! I had visited the restroom and placed my ring on the soap dispenser before I washed my hands!

"Mom!" I whispered frantically. "I left my ring in the restroom at the gas station!"

"We can't do anything about it now," she answered. "After the ceremony, we'll go back and look."

"After the ceremony!" my mind shouted. "It will be too late! Someone will have seen my ring and taken it, gloating in her good fortune."

The rest of the ceremony was a blur to me. I really didn't care who wed whom. I wanted my ring! Now!

It seemed like an eternity before the bride and groom

proceeded down the aisle to Mendelsohn's *Wedding March*, while smiling guests clapped to the music.

Mom, Dad, and I hurriedly got into the car and took the winding city streets to the thief-laden gas station. I jumped out of the car and headed for the restroom door that I had slammed behind me a couple of hours earlier. I noticed a young girl exiting the restroom with a grin as sly and deceptive as the Cheshire Cat's in *Alice in Wonderland*.

"Thief!" my heart shouted. "How dare you steal my ring!"

I flung open the door to the restroom and positioned myself in front of the huge gilded mirror with the silver-and-white soap dispenser beneath it. If the ring wasn't there, I would run after the girl with the cagey smile and demand my prized possession back! My heart literally stopped beating as I gazed down at the dispenser.

There it was in all its glory! My promise ring with its lustrous pearl in the center and the six sparkling diamonds around it. The silver-and-white coloring of my ring had blended into the silver-and-white of the soap dispenser. I was overjoyed with happiness and, at the same time, remorseful that I had even silently accused that innocent girl of stealing my ring.

Mom, Dad, and I headed for the freeway that would take us forty-five miles east of Los Angeles to our home in "our neck of the woods." I sat in the back seat of the car, dreaming of what my life would hold for me.

"With this ring I thee wed," my new husband would say to me as he placed a wedding ring on my finger. I pictured the beauty and sacredness of my new wedding ring touching the beauty and sacredness of my promise ring. These sacred symbols would forever remind me of a beautiful day in my life . . . and the many more beautiful days to come.

I would welcome the rays of each new dawn life would offer me . . . and be grateful for the promises of each new beginning.

What Happened When the Groom Was Misplaced

Carol McCracken

Augusta is having a panic attack," the text read. I flew up to the bride's dressing room.

Augusta, the bride, picked herself up off the floor where she had been lying in a crumpled heap. "It just hit me. All my bridesmaids left for the lineup and I was all alone, and I just realized the impact of what I'm getting ready to do," she told me and my assistant, Stacey, as she walked toward us.

Cautiously I asked, "Augusta, don't you want to get married?"

She gave an embarrassed giggle and wiped a tear away. "Oh, I want to get married so much! Someone has been with me the whole time and I guess I have been distracted with all the preparation. Maybe I just lost it. I need to get to my ceremony."

As a wedding planner, I am to make things go smoothly for the couple. Yet, years of experience have proved that something will always challenge the plan. It is just a matter of how you handle that challenge to the plan — like brides having panic attacks.

What Augusta didn't know, though, was at that very moment I had another problem. I didn't know where the groom was.

The day had been going well until a bit of rain had blown up. The ceremony for three hundred was to be outside. The bride and groom wanted pictures on the beach prior to the ceremony. That required trolley transportation from the ceremony area. Because the groom was not to see his bride, we had to carefully orchestrate the photography sessions.

As the bride and her ten bridesmaids and flower girl had boarded their trolley, a soft rain had begun.

The maid of honor and the photographer noticed the bride's expression of distress at the same time.

"Ladies change of plans," the photographer announced. "We'll take some pictures over here until the rain stops so we don't get behind schedule." She frantically texted me the update.

As the photographer texted me, the resort manager and I were discussing whether we needed to move the ceremony inside.

The mother of the groom walked by and insisted, "We *must* have the ceremony outside! There has been so much preparation and I am counting on hearing all the solos." Her ten-year-old son, the groom's brother, had been practicing for weeks for this gift to his brother. "I am going to start praying now, and the ceremony will be outside," she said.

"Yes, ma'am," I replied. "Then that is what we will do."

The DJ left for the ceremony area to move his equipment, just in case.

Another text from the photographer said that she had made up time because the rain had stopped. The bridesmaids had made it to the beach. Would I send the groomsmen to the beach now?

I smiled at the power of that prayer and went up with Stacey to pin on the boutonnieres and send the groomsmen to the beach for their pictures. Then Stacey and I hurried to the ceremony area to meet with the resort staff, and begin drying the chairs.

Another text from the bride's mother demanded my attention. "Augusta needs her handwritten vows and she can't find them. Are they with the items for the detail shots?"

I texted the photographer with the question. "Yes, I have them right here," came the reply.

"I'll take care of it!" I texted the bride's mother.

I ran to retrieve the vows from the photographer. Then, rushing into the elevator, I went up to where Augusta was getting ready, ran into the room where the maid of honor plucked them from my hand and said, "Oh, thank God, Augusta was stressing out!"

I jogged back to the ceremony area and began to dry a chair, breathing heavily from my jog.

Five minutes later another text arrived from the bride's mother. "You forgot to pick up the orange juice from my room for the rum punch. I'll send a family member down with it."

"Thanks," I replied, focusing on the speed of my chair drying.

Another text from the bride's mom came, "Lawrence can't find his cuff links, do you think those were with the items for the detail shots?"

"I'll check!" I texted back, beginning to sweat as the time for the ceremony to begin drew nearer and wet chairs stretched out before me.

I texted the photographer in the middle of her shoot and she replied, "The cufflinks were in the bag I returned to the room."

I texted her reply to the bride's mother as I was continuing to dry a chair. Guests were beginning to approach the area.

The bride's mother asked, "Can you take the cufflinks to the groom?"

"I need to get people seated right now," I replied.

"I'll get a runner to do it," she texted.

Thankful, I ended the call. I wrung out my seat-drying cloth, looked up, and to my relief saw that Stacey and the resort manager had finished drying the chairs. The ceremony area looked beautiful, as if rain had never happened.

A text came from the bride's mother telling me that the trolley was not picking up the groomsmen from the beach and they were so frustrated they were going to walk back to the ceremony area. I called the manager of the resort who investigated and told me that the trolley had broken down so she was going to get them.

It was now 5:45.

The bridal party was due to line up in five minutes.

And that's when I got the call from the bride's mother that Augusta was having the panic attack.

After sorting out the panic attack and confirming that Augusta was ready and willing to get married, we headed downstairs where she was going to hide with Stacey until I figured out through which entrance her groom would enter.

She did not need to know I had no idea where her groom was at that exact moment.

Hoping the resort manager had found the groomsmen, I tucked Augusta and Stacey in a corner and ran to the lineup area. Thank God! I saw groomsmen . . . but no groom.

"Has anyone seen Lawrence yet?" I asked with forced confidence.

"He's in the bathroom!" replied several groomsmen.

I ran to the men's restroom and boldly grabbed the hand of the unsuspecting groom on his way out. "I'm so very sorry for your transportation issue. Augusta is ready. Let's do this."

We rushed to the head of the lineup where I addressed the bridal party and honored guests.

"I know this has been stressful for everyone. You have had a lot of challenges. I am grateful to you and want to let you know that we are only three minutes behind schedule. Let's begin."

They all went obediently down the aisle. The seven-year-old ring bearer pulling his six-month-old cousin in a wagon stirred the hearts of the female portion of the crowd. I heard, "Look at that sweet baby! Aren't the two of them precious together?"

I ran and got the bride who was still hidden with Stacey as a lookout and brought her to the lineup area door. No one had turned the groom around so he wouldn't see her. So, I stopped short and the bride bumped into me, followed by Stacey, who was holding the "throw bouquet" for afterward, at the reception. Regaining my footing, I made turning around motions with my fingers for several seconds until the two officiants figured out what I wanted and turned the groom around.

The groom's ten-year-old brother sounded sweet and clear as he sang his solo.

I took the bride down the steps and positioned her so she was ready to walk down the aisle, then fluffed out her dress and veil one final time.

They turned the groom around to see his bride and he was transfixed.

She took a step forward . . . and her veil did not go with her. I caught it on the way down and replaced it. She started again . . .

and the veil apparently did not want to stay on her pretty head. It jerked off again. This time she told me she was done with the veil. She proceeded down the aisle to her groom without it.

There was silence. I thought the groom might be choked up. Then he began to sing to his bride. There was supposed to be music, but there was none; the rain had done something to the sound system. The unaccompanied voice of the groom filled the air. People began to tear up. He made it to the last note before his voice broke and he chuckled, put the microphone down and caught up his bride in a big hug.

How many grooms would do that for their bride?

Two people who were beautiful inside and out had one of the most meaningful ceremonies I had ever seen. They were meant to be together. The reception that followed was an outpouring of love as people danced and gave toasts under twinkling lights and crystal columns. The common theme seemed to be that everyone had known very early on that these two were destined for each other. They had chemistry. Literally.

A boy met a girl in organic chemistry class.

The bride, groom, and mother of the bride were not aware of everything that had been going on behind the scenes. Those days of preparation reminded me of how God works behind the scenes. He carefully orchestrates each moment of our lives. We have expectations and faith in the outcome. Sometimes the outcome isn't how we envision it. Fervent prayers for things to go a certain way are sometimes answered, just as when the groom's mother prayed for the ceremony not to be a wash out. That was in God's will.

For the wedding, the bride's mother had hired me and my

team so she could relax and enjoy the day with her daughter. She had no idea of all the things that were going on behind the scenes then, either. I was glad that she could be spared that stress.

How much stress is God sparing us from when we don't know what's going on behind the scenes of our lives?

We know that we will have trials in this world. They are to test us and develop our character.

It isn't every day you lose a groom in action. But God knew where he was the whole time. His purpose was to unite that exact groom with that exact bride. Perhaps it wasn't the way that I envisioned it, but it was the way that God wanted it.

This groom would do anything to get to his bride. He would have his wish fulfilled not to see her until she was adorned in her gorgeous bridal gown for him. He had faith, as did she. God put it together in a way that everyone would remember, and better than any of us had planned.

~ 6 ~

Tea Cakes

Tom Hooker

It's been six decades and more
since Grandma's tea cakes
first kissed my lips.
Perched in my high-chair,
I watched her concoct
those enchanting wafers:
blending ingredients, kneading dough,
flattening with rolling pin,
cutting disks with mayonnaise-jar lid.
Vanilla scent, lemon zest,
warm and sweet and ephemeral
cookie dissolving in my mouth.
It's been three decades and more
since Grandma's tea cakes
last kissed my lips.
Yet my tongue still
retains the indelible memory
of the evidence of Grandma's love.

My New Life

Norma C. Mezoe

It was my first Easter Sunday without my husband. As I looked around the church where my husband and I had worshiped and served together, I saw couples sitting closely side by side. The scene emphasized the undeniable fact that I was now alone.

It was to this church that my husband had been called to begin his first full-time ministry. He had given up the highest paying job he'd ever had to accept that position at the age of forty-five.

It was in this church that he began having an affair with a young wife who was the mother of two small children. It was from this church that they sped away in the darkness of midnight.

On that first Easter Sunday without my husband, the sermon was the joyful message of Christ's resurrection. It was a jubilant proclamation that the grave could not keep Jesus a prisoner. It was a promise that He had risen from the tomb to bring new life to all who would accept his gift.

As I sat alone that morning, I felt pain and loneliness, but I was also aware of the Lord's presence, and I experienced the joy of His Spirit as I accepted the new life He offered.

That's when I really realized I wasn't alone after all.

Romans 6:4b NIV promises just as Christ was raised from the dead through the glory of the Father, we too may live a new life.

If you are suffering a loss of any kind and are mourning that loss, take heart. Jesus will give you the assurance and the hope of new beginnings.

~ 8 ~

1 Survived
for Better or Purse

Annmarie B. Tait

Someone stole my car. That's the good news. The bad news is that it was wrapped around my purse when it disappeared.

A stolen car is sobering enough, but it's a skip in the park next to reaching for that life-support system identified by every woman as her purse, and realizing it's gone.

Just thinking about someone rifling through my personal um . . . stuff, sets my teeth on edge. E-gad! Right now my driver's license photo could be out there in some gutter frightening stray dogs and small children at play.

As if that isn't bad enough, I'm further burdened with calling one credit card company after another and reporting my cards stolen. The same organizations that not one month ago badgered me to purchase theft protection service. Amazingly enough several of the operators recalled me by name.

"Oh yes, Ms. Tait, I remember you. What's that? Someone stole your credit card? Oh my, how unfortunate. Makes you wish you hadn't blown raspberries in my ear, and slammed the phone down two weeks ago doesn't it?"

I responded sheepishly, and ordered new cards complete with the deluxe theft protection service — perpetual plan.

I'm proud to report that my credit cards are protected against theft from now until five years after my death.

Sensing only a slight rise in my blood pressure, I forged ahead and tackled the DMV about replacing my license. Big mistake. Glancing at the first item on the form pushed my blood pressure through the roof.

The form read: "Please state your driver's license number in the space provided." Were they joking? They couldn't possibly be ludicrous enough to think I'd memorized it. My "important numbers" memory bank was already overloaded with other critical information . . . like my bankcard PIN, my employee ID, my cell phone number, my five plus four zip code, and the local pizza delivery phone number. Now there's an important number.

I ask you, who the heck knows their driver's license number by heart?

I looked up at the snickering DMV employee as he rolled his soggy unlit cigar from one side of his mouth to the other.

"Excuse me sir. If I give you my social security number can you look up my driver's license number in your computer?"

He sighed disgustedly then replied, "Every teary-eyed dame that walks in this joint asks the same question. No lady, I can't. Either you know the number or forget it."

"Well if we're all asking the same question, might you suggest the idea to your boss?"

He snarled then said, "I am not paid to make suggestions. I am paid to process the form, which I can't do unless it's filled out correctly.

I huffed over to the waiting area then plopped down with the form in hand. I dialed my husband's phone number and was relieved when he picked up. I knew Mr. Organization would have that number recorded somewhere, and he did not disappoint. Grudgingly I completed the form and handed it to the clerk.

While waiting for my husband to arrive and take me home, I thought of nothing but the treasures hidden in the crevices of my purse and wallet — treasures I'd never see again. Irreplaceable photos, the last little note my grandmother wrote me just before she passed away, an antique brooch I'd intended to take to the jeweler that day for repair. All gone forever. Even the wallet itself, tattered and worn. bore very special meaning to me. I'd purchased it in Holland when I was twenty-one and my best friend and I had taken our first self-funded unchaperoned vacation. This personal badge of independence had now vanished forever.

After squeezing every last drop of self-pity from my pout fest, it was time to get down to business.

First, I fished out another purse from my closet. Then I chose a wallet from my vast collection of sparkling new ones, all gifts from anyone who ever caught sight of my old tattered wallet from Holland, and all still in their boxes.

Next I threw in a packet of tissues, a pen, a comb, my keys, and my cell phone. Out the door and off to work. Life goes on.

A few weeks have passed since my harrowing experience with crime. The car remains at large along with the thief. Most likely we'll hear of neither again. I can deal with it.

The insurance is settled and delivery on my new car is scheduled for next week. My new theft-protected credit cards are nestled in the folds of my current wallet and the DMV came through with a brand new driver's license.

Today I reached in my desk drawer and pulled out my purse, amazed at how heavy it was. Ah, nature has taken its course and life is back to normal.

My wallet from Holland is gone but not my memories of that trip. The pictures are also gone, but not from my heart where I keep them safely tucked away and view them regularly.

It just goes to show you that the really important possessions in life can never be lost or stolen. Everything else can be replaced.

I would love to recover that old wallet, but if I don't, I can use a brand new wallet every year for the rest of my life and never have to buy one. If you ever have to deal with a stolen purse, relax. I promise you, you'll survive. Everything happens for a reason, so "they" say.

Who are "they" you ask.

The purse and wallet manufacturers I suppose.

~ 9 ~

Glorious Day

Bob Blundell

The azure waters of the Sea of Galilee shimmered in the early morning sunlight. A fine silver mist hovered above the surface, partially obscuring the mountains on the opposite shore. I stood on the western bank, absorbing the beauty that lay before me, and quietly pondered its significance.

As written of in the last chapter of John's Gospel, this is where Jesus showed himself to his disciples as they fished from their tiny boat along the beach near Tiberias.

A crisp easterly breeze washed over my face, and I could almost smell the scent of a charcoal fire and freshly cooked fish. I closed my eyes and listened, imagining the joy and laughter in the disciples' voices as they huddled around Jesus, sharing a final meal with the one who had chosen them to change the world. As my mind pondered the moment, I could see it unfold before me.

* * *

The darkness of night had faded and a cool breeze pushed gentle swells across the sea, slapping the hull of the small fishing boat. Rocking back and forth, it strained against its anchor, and the aged cedar planks creaked, piercing the silence of the early morning. A tattered sail hanging from the mast popped and swung against the sides of the wooden post as occasional gusts of wind breathed life into the hand-sewn cloth.

Hearing the snap of the sail, Peter sat up from where he lay curled on the bottom of the boat.

A gull swooped down near the water, then cried out as it accelerated into the sky. Looking up, Peter noticed the sun had crested the horizon. He rubbed his tired eyes and leaned against the rail, peering into the silvery mist hovering just above the surface of the sea.

He and the other men had fished most of the night, and after tending the nets for hours and being weary from their work, allowed blessed sleep to overtake them. Peter stood and moved to the bow. He took a long drink from a gourd containing fresh water and found a small goatskin bag containing several dates. He chewed a date slowly, savoring its sweetness as he watched the sun begin its journey above the sea.

The sight of the morning sun glistening on the water brought back fond memories of his father taking him fishing as a boy, teaching him to work the nets as his father before him had been taught. But deep within him there was a sadness that clung to him like a dark veil. A horrible feeling of loss. He had denied and forsaken the man whom he adored and had sworn to follow, no matter what.

Three years before, he had been told to follow Him, and he had left the life he knew and obeyed, not fully understanding the power compelling him, but willing to learn as an apt pupil seeking knowledge from his Teacher. Yet despite what he had been taught and the miracles he had witnessed, Peter had betrayed Him. He knew it was fear that caused him to turn his back on his Teacher. But fear of what? Hadn't this man taught him that suffering in this life was inevitable? He felt moist tears on his cheeks, wished he could change the past, but knew in his heart he would have to live with the terrible injustice he had committed.

The others began to stir. "Wake up, men," Peter said. "It's time to sail back to port."

His brother, Andrew, rolled over on his back and smiled. "Perhaps you will prepare our breakfast before we sail." The others laughed along with him.

Although Peter laughed too, thoughts of the previous weeks weighed heavily upon him. The Teacher had said He would be leaving and that Peter, an ordinary fisherman would take His place. Peter had scarcely felt worthy of following such a cause, much less leading it, and he initially refused. But after his eyes were opened to who the Teacher truly was, he prayed he would be granted the wisdom and courage to accomplish the daunting task he had been given.

After that, Peter had failed when he denied even knowing the Lord. Surely, he had lost the chance to serve the Master in any meaningful way.

As the brothers conversed, Peter gazed toward the grey rocky shore fifty yards away and as the mist began to lift, he saw a man, wearing a pale white robe, walking along the shoreline. Behind him a small fire burned and plumes of grey smoke swirled into the thick air. The man waved and called out, "Have you caught anything during the night?"

"No," Peter replied, wearily.

"Fish on the right side of the boat," the man said.

The brothers looked quizzically at the stranger on the shore and then at Peter, who shrugged. "Do as he said."

Two of the disciples lifted the nets from the bottom of the craft and another pulled the anchor from its mooring. In seconds, a breath of wind filled the small sail and the boat slowly tracked to the east. They had scarcely moved twenty yards when the nets became taut.

Andrew leaned over the edge of the craft staring into the azure water. "The nets!" he exclaimed. "They're full of fish. Help me pull them in."

As the men excitedly moved to the right side of the boat to lift the nets, one of the brothers gazed at the man standing on the shore. Surprise crossed his face. "It's the Lord!" he cried excitedly.

Peter recognized the Messiah, and in his exuberance, he leaped into the sea. He treaded water until he was able to walk to the shore and when he reached his Savior, he knelt at his feet, feeling an immense joy wash over him like a huge wave.

"My Lord," he cried, his heart filled with joy. "You have returned again!"

"Come, Simon Peter," Jesus said. "Join me at the fire. I have prepared fish for all of you."

Jesus and the disciples sat around a charcoal fire, eating breakfast and reminiscing of days past.

Though they knew there would be hardships and suffering in the days and years to come, their hearts were pure and full of joy and peace. When the meal was finished, Jesus took Peter a few yards away from the others. He placed his hands on Peter's head and kissed his forehead. Then he blessed Peter with the gift of forgiveness and the power of the Holy Spirit that would enable him to find the strength and courage to accomplish the enormous task ahead of him.

* * *

The vision began to fade, and I squinted into the amber glare of the sun, my mind returning to the present. This beach, this incredible place, exuded an air of holiness and purity, and I felt unworthy standing on the same shore where our Lord and his disciples had walked.

I looked at the small oblong stone I held in my hand. It was like any ordinary stone, grey in color, except this one came from the rocky shore where I stood. I turned it over, examining it carefully, feeling its hard edges, then closed it in my fist. I sensed its significance, knowing I must never lose it or the memory of this sacred moment.

Rain, Pelicans, Chocolate...

Terri Elders

At times, our own light goes out and is rekindled
by a spark from another person.

Albert Schweitzer

Sue, the yoga teacher at my senior living complex, incorporated the theme of gratitude into our sessions. She asked that we clear our minds of troubling thoughts about a past that can't be undone and a future that can't be predicted.

"Think about this moment," she would say. "Let's begin by giving thanks for this morning's gorgeous sunrise, and the beauty of our surroundings."

One morning, though, I blinked back a tear. "What difference does it make whether there's a nice sunrise or not?" I thought to myself. "Who even cares?" I tried to follow Sue's instructions to empty my mind of negativity. But when I leaned forward as we concluded our session, clasping my hands in "Namaste," I noticed how they trembled. I'd been shaking intermittently with anger and grief since my daughter-in-law had died a week earlier.

Mari Lou had been only fifty-three, with everything to look forward to. She'd recently reached an agreement with a major publishing house for publication of her first young adult novel. She'd celebrated the good news with her Tuesday morning writing group, to which I belonged, by toasting to its success with hard-to-find classic Nehi Orange Soda. Her fictional heroine, Possum, who lived in the in the South during the 1930s, drank it. Orange, too, had always been Mari Lou's favorite color. She'd even bought an orange handbag for her expected book tour.

She'd been preparing for a stay at a friend's desert condo in Indian Wells to finish her final edits. Her clothes and provisions were packed. My son, Steve, had planned to drive her there, but she felt so ill she'd asked to go to an ER instead. She was jaundiced and so was admitted to the hospital. Over the next week she underwent a series of biopsies. After a month's stay in ICU, she'd succumbed to complications from a combination of a previously undetected heart defect and lymphoma.

Steve, Mari Lou's mom, Maria, and I had taken turns staying with her in her hospital room, so she'd never be left unattended. It was on my watch that she drew her final, labored breaths.

In yoga class shortly afteward, as Sue suggested we be grateful that we could inhale purifying air, I remembered how Mari Lou's own breathing had become such torture for her in her final days. What was there to be grateful about?

I'd always comforted myself by remembering it's always darkest before the dawn. Now I doubted that. Each new day seemed even darker. I even woke up wondering what would go wrong next. Sure enough, my negative expectations managed to be met.

I'd taken my car in for a routine oil change and learned that it needed new tires and brakes, expenses I could barely afford. Several people I'd been friendly with began to look the other way as I passed them in the halls of my apartment complex. My email inbox filled with a flurry of rejections for stories I'd submitted. I even noticed a hole in the shoulder of the dress I planned to wear to Mari Lou's memorial service.

Nothing went right.

Not only did I grieve Mari Lou, I also grieved the loss of my ability to look forward to each new day. I no longer expected to experience joy. Life seemed devoid of purpose.

Finally, I began to help my son tidy his house that had gone neglected during Mari Lou's illness. I cleaned out several kitchen cupboards, and wandered into the den. There, on the sofa I noticed a box with items that my daughter-in-law had packed in preparation for that prospective trip to her desert retreat.

Idly, I began sorting through it. Beneath some boxes of Girl Scout Tagalongs, I discovered a faded, frayed black notebook. Its cover bore stickers featuring a variety of Dr. Seuss characters. Its label read "My Book about Me."

Mari Lou had begun keeping it during a dark period of her life, apparently. In one entry dated a decade earlier, I saw "Things I Am Grateful For." She listed, "The luxury of saying I hate my life." Following that single negative comment, though, I read the things she loved: rain, pelicans, chocolate, cats, Steve.

On following pages, she gave thanks for her writing and editing talents, and for her ability to appreciate ballet, the theater, and the arts. Every page, though, included the basics: rain, pelicans, chocolate, cats, Steve.

That evening I sat down and opened a blank notebook of my own. Even at my advanced age, it's not too late to begin my book about me, I reasoned. So, I began my own gratitude list.

Remembering the harrowing hospital days, I wrote how grateful I was to see Father John in the visitor's lounge a few days before Mari Lou died. He'd stopped to watch the television news showing Pope Francis visiting St. Patrick's Cathedral.

I'd approached him. "Excuse me, Father," I began. "My daughter-in-law is on life support in the ICU, and her mother, who is Catholic, has been hoping a priest would drop by to pray for her."

"I'll go there with you immediately," he'd said.

I'm grateful that he gave Mari Lou sacraments, thus comforting her mom.

An old friend, who had sent me a stuffed bear when my husband had died, surprised me again by sending another, something new to hug. I also remembered the kind words and condolence cards I'd received from other unexpected sources.

I'd been grateful that Mari Lou's publisher attended her memorial and promised a big launch for her book on its release. I'd been grateful I was able to cover that hole in my dress with an orange-beaded pendant Steve had given me for Mother's Day when he was about ten years old.

I'd been grateful that my son had started to see a bereavement counselor, and that he continued to be in touch with Mari Lou's writing group students. I'd been thankful he'd planned to spend Christmas with her mom and me.

Most of all, I'm grateful that Mari Lou kept her gratitude journal so that I could learn how much pleasure she had derived from rain, pelicans, chocolate . . . and my son. And that finding that well-worn notebook had rekindled my spark and enabled me to find what I thought I had lost.

I even returned to yoga class.

"Let's begin by giving thanks for this beautiful warm morning," Sue began. I smiled.

When we concluded, we bowed, murmuring, "Namaste." As I clasped my hands before my heart, I noted that my body no longer trembled. Sorrow remained with me, of course, but anger had been quelled.

I continue even now to be grateful that I, too, live in a world with rain, pelicans, chocolate . . . and my son. I'm grateful for the sunrise, and for rekindled joy in God's creations.

11

Little Girl Lost

Lynn Mosher

In 1981, six-year-old Adam Walsh was abducted from a mall in Florida. Two weeks later, the authorities found the gruesome proof of his death.

Right after the abduction of Adam Walsh, I lost my five-year-old daughter in a large department store at a mall. To say I was freaked out would be an understatement.

Over the years we have given our sweet daughter many nicknames. I'll just use one: Merf.

As we were shopping, I was looking around in one of the women's departments. Merf loved to feel fabrics, especially soft ones, and would occasionally crawl under the clothes on the racks and feel the fabrics. Thinking she was right beside me, or under a rack, I said something to her.

But she didn't answer me.

I called to her.

No answer.

I looked around, and under, and called again.

No answer.

Starting to panic, I called a little louder.

No answer.

Now getting desperate, I yelled out in the store for her, but she still did not answer.

With my heart pumping so hard I thought it would jump out of my body, my mind raced through all the horrific scenarios that could happen.

"Oh, God! Help!" I prayed.

As I frantically searched everywhere for her, I heard someone calling my name from somewhere within the store . . . "LYNN!"

I looked around and saw a very dear friend coming through the entrance of the store. I waved to her.

From halfway across the store, she yelled, "Are you looking for Merf?"

"YES! Where is she?"

"She's right here by the door!"

I ran to get her.

After smothering my daughter with kisses and practically squishing her insides out with my hug, I asked her why she hadn't stayed by my side.

She said she couldn't find me and, because she knew which way we had come in, she went to the double set of doors and waited in between them because she knew I would come out that way.

Oh, be still my heart! It still shakes me up to this day.

With all the evil in the world, it is important that we teach our children and grandchildren to stay close to us, or whoever is in charge of them at the moment. We want to teach them with love and gentleness so we do not scare them. However, a little apprehension is a good thing.

And, at the same time we explain closeness to them, we need to teach them that staying close to the Lord, as our heavenly

Father, is of utmost importance. As His children, we are never alone or without His help in any situation.

When Jehovah-shammah (Lord is present) came as Immanuel (God with us), He said, *"I am with you always."* (Matthew 28:20) *God is our refuge and strength, an ever-present help in trouble.* (Psalm 46:1 NIV)

NOTE: In 2006, on the twenty-fifth anniversary of Adam's death, President George W. Bush signed into law the federal statute called the Adam Walsh Child Protection and Safety Act, which also created the sex offender registry.

12

All Is Not Lost

Helen L. Hoover

Cyndi, my son's friend, liked antiques, quilts, and hand-crafted items. For a young woman, this was a little unusual, but she was an unusually delightful person. I enjoyed the time spent with her when she was at our home with our son.

When I saw sweatshirts embellished with old quilt squares at a craft fair. I immediately knew such a gift would be a great one for Cyndi. Although her birthday was several months away, I went ahead with the project. After it was completed, I showed it to my son and my husband, who both thought she would enjoy the item. Then I put it in storage until time for her birthday.

I'd enjoyed making it from old quilt pieces I had and I felt confident that this was a gift she would like. Pleased, I didn't need to think about it anymore.

The months passed. A couple of days before Cyndi's birthday, I went to get the sweatshirt so I could wrap it. I looked where I was sure I had stored it.

I couldn't find it.

I looked on all shelves in the closet, and on the closet floor. I looked in dresser drawers. I looked in the linen closet.

Oh my, where could it be?

"Do you know where I stored the sweatshirt for Cyndi?" I asked my son and husband.

"No, where did you put it? My husband replied.

"Well, that does seem to be the problem. I can't find it. Now what will I do?"

I continued to look until her birthday — no sweatshirt. There was nothing else to do except confess that I'd lost her gift.

"Cyndi, I made you a special present, but I can't find it. It has to be here somewhere in the house. It's a sweatshirt with a quilt block sewn into the front. When I find it, I'll let you know. I'm so sorry."

"Oh, don't worry," she said. "It sounds wonderful."

A couple more months went by and during those months the sweatshirt was on my mind almost continually. *Where could it be?*

One day, while restacking clothes on a shelf in the closet, there was the sweatshirt. *Hallelujah!* I almost jumped and touched the ceiling. Relief flooded through me. At last, I could give it to her.

She did like it and remained considerate about me losing it. I was also looking forward to a possible long-term relationship with her as a daughter-in-law. However, that didn't turn out to be the plan for her and my son. They decided to go their separate ways.

"Cyndi, even though you won't be part of our family," I told her, "I don't want to lose you as a friend."

"Yes, I agree," she said. "Remaining as friends is my goal too."

And we have. It has been twenty-five years since that incident. We have maintained contact with each other and occasionally have a personal visit.

I'm glad that although I lost her sweatshirt for a few months, I didn't lose her as a friend.

13

Coffee Connection

Laura Taylor

Nothing urgent beckoned me on this quiet morning. Birds chirped their merry melodies. Trees danced in the gentle breeze. My soul smiled at the thought of unhurried coffee and conversation with Jesus. I popped a pod in the Keurig and listened in anticipation as it buzzed, gurgled, and dripped each delightful drop into my mug.

Inhaling the steamy deliciousness of a perfectly brewed cup of coffee, I grabbed my Bible and journal, and headed toward the patio. Sliding the door open, the freshness of a new morning invited me to bask in the presence of the Creator.

I settled into my favorite spot, opened my Bible, and reached for that perfect cup of coffee. It wasn't there. Somewhere on the trip outside, I'd set my cup down.

This minor inconvenience couldn't quench the joy bubbling in my soul. I strolled back to my desk. It wasn't there. Joy unshaken, I decided to retrace my steps. It was a solid plan, and something I had become adept at through the years.

Humming that sweet childhood tune, "I've got the joy, joy, joy, joy down in my heart," I turned toward the door when a rude realization stopped me.

I didn't remember my steps.

Pondering this new dilemma, I decided on a different tactic: I would journey back to the beginning — back to my Keurig. Feet dancing in time with that happy tune, I was off to find my missing coffee cup.

The Keurig, sitting proud and empty, seemed to wink at me in amusement. Annoyed but undeterred, I was determined to find my coffee cup and return to the peacefulness of time outside with God. Three laps around the kitchen island, a peek inside the air fryer (just in case), and a trek to the bathroom all came up empty.

The joyous ode to my perfect morning waned.

My heart, which had been beating in time with the restful rhythm of Spring, now thumped like the bass drum in a marching band. This casual jaunt to retrieve a misplaced coffee cup had turned into a full blown, cardiac quest to uncover the holy grail. I was not prepared for this. Especially without the assistance of caffeine.

Undaunted, I plumbed the depths of cabinets and appliances. Even the dog's kennel. "If only you could remember your steps," my brain chastised. Unbelievable! Coffee cups don't just vanish.

Thirty minutes into this impromptu adventure, I changed tactics and shoved a new pod into the Keurig. This time the whirring and buzzing of that delightful device felt like the sound of defeat.

As the last drop of coffee dripped its way into the mug, a Bible verse trickled into my brain. *You have circled this mountain long enough. Now, turn. . . .* (Deuteronomy 2:3 NASB). Wondering if this was a divine revelation, I turned around, scanning countertops in every direction. Nothing. I raised the freshly brewed coffee to my lips and laughed, "Okay, Lord, I sense there might be a greater lesson here than a lost coffee cup."

My curiosity piqued, I decided to find the verse and read the rest of the story. Settling back into my favorite spot, coffee cup firmly in my grasp, I turned to the book of Deuteronomy: Moses' farewell address to the nation of Israel.

As he stood gazing out at this new generation poised to enter the Promised Land, Moses knew that he wouldn't be going with them. I could almost feel the heaviness of these final words pressing on his heart. He had led, loved, and longed over this stubborn people for forty years.

During that time, they wept and waited. They rebelled then repented. They murmured then marveled. They allowed their fear to dictate what their faith should have settled: God requires obedience; God blesses obedience; and God is always faithful.

Eyes fixed upon that land flowing with milk and honey, they realized their wandering had not been in vain. God was there every step of the way.

Moses knew the history of his people and their tendency toward fear and rebellion. He understood the weight of his final message. His final words invited them on a journey to reflect on their years of wandering. He implored them to remember their sins and God's faithfulness. Finally, he called on them to renew their commitment of obedience to God in all things.

Closing my Bible, I thought about the mystery of my missing coffee cup and God's nudge to "turn." It was then I realized this was God's invitation for me to reflect upon the wilderness wanderings of my own life.

I retraced the moments that I'd entered relationships that

didn't honor Him. I recalled the times I gave in to fear when God called me to stay the course during a difficult and lonely season far away from home. My past rose within me like a flood: words spoken and regretted, resentment chosen over forgiveness, and moments of ministry that I missed.

Before the waters of emotion could overwhelm me, my mind turned to reflect upon the faithfulness of God. God, who in His goodness, never wasted one of those painful or rebellious moments. I sat in silent awe at His incredible kindness. A soft light of realization dawned within me. Just as with those wilderness wanderers, God had been with me through every step and misstep of my own journey.

In the stillness of that moment, my heart smiled as I heard the tender whisper of the Father inviting me to renew my commitment to His Word and His ways. That sweet childhood tune began to reverberate through me once again, "I've got the joy, joy, joy, joy down in my heart."

As I headed back inside, something caught my eye. It was that errant coffee cup beaming at me from a windowsill. I must have placed it there when I paused to open the blinds. Chuckling, I found myself delighted, again, by the tenderness of a God who turned the search for a missing coffee cup into a sweet reminder of His faithful love that can never be lost or misplaced.

~ 14 ~

Just Follow the Light

Lola Di Giulio De Maci

I stared at the miles of road ahead and wondered if we would ever get there. My husband navigated our Oldsmobile in and out of freeway traffic as our seven-year-old daughter and four-year-old son slept soundly in the back seat. I anxiously counted the number of exits before we would arrive at the California beach town we would visit for a week. If I closed my eyes and listened, I could hear the sounds of the ocean's waves rhythmically splashing along the shore. I welcomed the peaceful invitation.

I was lost. Adrift in a sea of pain.

I had recently lost my third child, a baby girl, who arrived with wisps of light blond curls and ten perfect, baby-pink toes. She had tiptoed into my life on a warm August evening and then left as quickly as she had come, seeing the light of only one morning.

She had lived barely a day, but in my heart, she had lived a lifetime. I named her Angela.

"Let's go somewhere near the ocean," my husband had said. "We can sit on the beach and watch the kids play. We can talk about where we go from here. What do you think?"

I agreed. It sounded soothing to my shattered soul.

The ocean was our getaway during the day. I could get lost in its peaceful vibes and somehow cope with my grief. But evening was the hardest. When the sun started to dip behind the horizon, my mind revisited that warm August evening and the tears came.

On the way back from the beach at suppertime, my husband would drive us to a small deli we had discovered not far from our motel.

"I'll be right back," he said after taking our orders one particular evening. He disappeared inside. Staring into nowhere, I sat motionless, in the front seat of the car and waited while my son and daughter sat quietly behind me.

As neon lights of the delicatessen blinked off and on before me, a young woman with a mass of blond curls appeared at the car window just a few inches from me, interrupting my reverie.

"There's a festival going on down the street," she said. "You might want to go there. They have hot dogs, cotton candy, rides, games, and so much more. Just follow the lights down the road to the edge of town. You can't miss it." She smiled and then disappeared as quickly as she had come.

Evening had now slipped into night and I was in no mood for cotton candy, rides, or games. So we went back to the motel and ended our day at the beach.

Over the days and weeks that followed, I kept thinking of that young woman with the mass of blond curls, who seemed to appear out of nowhere. Why had she been she at the deli at the moment that I was there? Where had she come from?

"There's a festival going on down the street," she had said. "Just follow the lights down the road. You can't miss it."

What she had said took on new meaning for me.

Slowly I began putting one foot in front of the other, and the simple pleasures that had once made me happy started to appear again. I began uncovering little pieces of joy that were just waiting to be resurrected.

I eventually found my way back to the festival of my life by following the lights down the road to a brighter day. I'm so glad I didn't miss the journey. I would have missed out on so much of my life and the lives of my three children — the two that live with me here on Earth, and the one that lives with God in Heaven.

And finally, I found peace in my heart and in evening's shadows.

~ 15 ~

Orphaned, But Not Alone

Tanja Dufrene

I came across an invitation for writers to submit devotions about the goodness of God. Specific scriptures were listed from which to choose. Scanning the list I noticed 1 Chronicles 1 was still available. I quickly read the chapter and thought, *That's a strange passage to write about since it is a chapter listing genealogy records.* Occasionally, a few words were penned about an individual, such as being a mighty warrior or chief. *No wonder no one else has signed up for this one.* Yet for some reason, I was drawn to it.

Soon thereafter, I recalled a recent conversation with a dear friend. "I feel like an orphan," she said. Now in her seventies, she had said her final goodbye to her parents. No longer would she enjoy visits with them or make more memories. Their time on earth was finished. Memorial services had been held in their honor and their remains lay still in the earth.

Hers had been a close-knit family with all that such relationships can bring, including both celebrations and challenges. Since we had spent much time together, she had shared many stories of their joys and sorrows. Yet now she would face the rest of her days without them. She grieved and felt lost — alone and orphaned.

Our conversation rolled around in my head for days as I recalled other people I knew to be social orphans, and what I had read about their situations.

"In contrast to a biological orphan, a social orphan may have living parents, but due to drug addiction, abandonment, poverty, etc. the parents are not able to handle their responsibilities, forcing the child to find a sense of home and love somewhere else," Matthew Barber wrote.[1]

And Drs. Henry Cloud and John Townsend wrote: "God has designed us to grow up in godly families where parents do the things he has commanded. They nurture us, they have good boundaries, they forgive and help us resolve the split between good and bad, and they empower us to become responsible adults. But many people have not had this experience. They are psychological orphans who need to be adopted and cared for by the body of Christ; to differing extents, this is true of all of us."[2]

These thoughts weighed heavy in my mind as I considered the emotional pain experienced by so many in the body of Christ, and our immense responsibility to show compassion and care.

It was then that I remembered what Jesus said: *"If you love me, you will obey what I command. And I will ask the Father, and he will give you another Counselor to be with you forever – the Spirit of truth. The world cannot accept him, because it neither sees him nor knows him. But you know him, for he lives with you and will be in you. I will not leave you as orphans; I will come to you."* (John 14:15-18 NIV)

I will not leave you as orphans. The words washed over my soul, seeped into my mind and soothed my aching heart. My words, my actions, my reasoning and rationalizations were simply too inadequate to comfort my hurting friends. Yet, I have a Friend who knows and cares for my friends who are suffering the loneliness and sadness of feeling orphaned.

God's Word includes a detailed genealogical record of ancient peoples, a heartwarming reminder that He knows us each by name, and He said He would not leave us as orphans.

So as we travel through our days, let us remember to interact gently with one another. Many are orphans, and in varying ways: Some are physically orphaned while others may be socially, psychologically, or emotionally orphaned.

Perhaps there are those around us whom we might adopt for a season. Perhaps there are even those who have adopted us along the way, helping us become who we are today.

Religion that God our Father accepts as pure and faultless is this: to look after orphans and widows in their distress and to keep oneself from being polluted by the world. (James 1:27 NIV)

[1] Barber, Matthew. "What Does it Mean to Be an Orphan?" *Hope Unlimited – for Children.* https://hopeunlimited.org/what-does-it-mean-to-be-an orphan/#:~:text=Although%20many%20recognize%20an%20orphan,their%20own%20meanings%20and%20implications. Retrieved: 16 Apr 2023.

[2] Drs. Cloud, Henry & Townsend, John. *Boundaries.* Grand Rapids, MI: Zondervan Publishing. 1992.

~ 16 ~

Never Take Candy
from a Baby

Carol Graham

Is there a Murphy's Law that says: When you are dressed to the
nines, mishaps or mini disasters will happen?

My daughter, her two children, my husband, and I had
attended the Celebration of Life service for a dear friend of ours.
It was difficult for all of us because we had lost someone who had
been a close friend to our entire family for thirty-five years. We
knew he was with Jesus, but all of us would dearly miss him.

The day was exceptionally hot and we were eager to get home.
My husband sat in the far rear seat of my daughter Rochelle's
SUV facing our one-year-old granddaughter, Brie, who sat in
her car seat. Hubby was entertaining Brie, who was giggling and
having a great time with Papa.

Each of us was deep in thought regarding the day's events
when hubby shouted, "Why did you give her chocolate?"

"What chocolate? I didn't give her any chocolate," Rochelle
replied. "William, did you give your sister some chocolate?"

"MOM, it isn't chocolate. It's POO!" was his response.

Brie had been cleaning out her diaper and handing

the contents to Papa. She thought it was a great game. Papa . . . not so much.

It was too late. He had already taken some "chocolate" from his granddaughter.

We were on a busy highway with narrow shoulders that didn't allow much room to stop our vehicle or clean the baby and the car. And remember, we were all dressed up, it was hot outside, and all we had to use for cleanup were some baby wipes. No water. Not even a bag in which to place the deposits.

Rochelle stripped the clothes off of Brie and put them on the side of the highway — which I protested for a moment. "Mom, do you want to hold them in your lap the rest of the way home?"

Thoughts of the odor wafting through the car made me gag.

After we placed Brie on the driver's seat, it was my job to clean her, her hair, under her nails — everywhere. Rochelle's job was to clean the entire car seat, the window, the door, and the floor.

All with one box of baby wipes.

We could only open the car door partway because of a cement barricade on the edge of the highway shoulder.

Amazingly, we were able to do a thorough enough job to get us the rest of the way home, which was a five-hour drive.

Considering all the emotions of that day, the moment that will be etched into my mind's eye forever was the look on Papa's face when he realized, "This ain't chocolate!"

The tears we'd shed earlier that day over the loss of our friend were replaced by laughter.

And the moral of this story? Never take candy from a baby!

17

The Day I Lost the Parade

Ellen Andersen

I t was December 1981. I was twelve years old, I played the clarinet in the band at Joe Walker Junior High School. I was excited because this was the first year I would get to march in the Lancaster Christmas Parade. I'd been in a few parades before, but this was different. This was a big parade. There would be more people watching, and the route was longer. The band had been practicing for three months to memorize our music, march in step, and form straight ranks and files. Ready or not, it was time for the parade.

Our uniforms were navy blue pants with matching jackets. A red and white overlay with a large JW covered our chests from shoulder to waist. We wore uncomfortable, shiny black shoes with white spats. We also wore white shakos (caps) about ten to twelve inches high. It was extremely hot, even in December. We lived in the high desert where "Winter" existed in name only.

My folks were out of town that weekend so I'd made arrangements for my aunt and uncle to drop me off at the beginning of the parade, then I would get a ride home with Debbie, another girl in the band. Debbie lived just three blocks up the street from me and her parents would be in town so they had agreed to give me a ride.

The parade route ran about a mile and a half down Lancaster Boulevard and then turned a corner to the left where we dispersed. Debbie and I had agreed to meet after the parade at the local Sav-On, a drugstore back on Lancaster Boulevard. So after the parade, I dismantled my instrument and headed back to the parade route. It had taken me longer to put my instrument away than it had for Debbie so she left before I did.

I hadn't paid attention to how far the band had gone after we turned the corner, but I figured I'd see the rest of the parade coming. I walked and walked and eventually realized something was wrong. *Why haven't I come to the parade yet?* I wondered. *It wasn't that far.*

After walking three or four blocks, I began to notice there were houses lining the street. Lancaster Boulevard is lined with businesses. It didn't make sense. I wondered if I'd actually passed it somehow. It was a crazy thought. How could I have passed the parade? It would've been obvious when I'd reached it, wouldn't it?

Finally, after having walked about a quarter of a mile, I realized I was lost. I turned around and headed back up the street hoping to find the parade. I must have looked ridiculous walking in my band uniform — overlay, blue jacket and matching pants, shako, black shoes and spats — and carrying my instrument case through a residential neighborhood.

I was alone. No people or cars around. Part of me hoped I'd find somebody so I could ask them where I was. On the other hand, I was a bit relieved that no one had seen me lost looking like that. Yet despite my determination not to cry, after ten or fifteen minutes of walking, my muscles had tensed up and tears flowed.

At last! I found the street.

The only problem was . . . the parade was over by then!

I didn't worry too much about it, and just went to Sav-On where Debbie and I had agreed to meet. I assumed she and her parents would be there waiting for me. I walked in and went up and down each aisle looking and calling out for her.

"Debbie? Debbie?"

Where was she? I couldn't see her anywhere. I went back and checked each aisle again.

Where was she and where were her parents?

Finally, I approached one of the employees.

"I'm looking for my friend and her parents. Have you seen anyone looking for me?" I asked

"What does your friend look like?' the lady replied.

"She has long, blond hair with wings," I told her.

"Sorry, I haven't seen anyone like that," she said.

Then I began to really get scared.

Now what was I going to do? My parents weren't home, and I didn't have a ride. I was about six or seven miles from home — way too far to walk, especially in this heat. I went back outside and looked around, hoping to find an adult who could help me.

A policeman spotted me, saw me crying, and asked what was wrong. I'd been taught that the police were there to help you so I told him, "I can't get home. My friend was supposed to drive me home from the parade today and I can't find her."

"Where were you supposed to meet her?" he asked

"Sav-On, but I just went there and she's not there," I said.

"Well, let's go back and see if we can find her together," he suggested.

We went back, even though I was pretty sure we wouldn't

find her there. I was right.

Then the policeman asked, "Is there anyone else you can call?"

"I don't know," I told him. "My parents are gone until tonight. That's why I was supposed to ride home with my friend. Maybe we could call my aunt and uncle, but I don't even know if they're home this afternoon. They dropped me off this morning but I don't know if they're there now."

Cell phones didn't exist yet, so the officer said he'd take me to the police station where I could call my aunt or uncle and have them pick me up.

Still scared, I nodded my head, uncertainly. I didn't know what we'd do if they weren't home.

I got in the police car, in the *back seat* of the car. *Oh my gosh, this is where the criminals sit!* I thought. I ducked, not wanting anyone to see me and think I'd broken the law. And I began to cry as quietly as I could.

When we got to the police station, the officer took me into a back room. I looked around to see if anyone was there in handcuffs. I'd never been in a police station before. I didn't see anyone who'd been arrested, so I relaxed a little and tried not to cry. The policeman who'd picked me up asked for my aunt and uncle's names and their phone number.

"Margaret and Jim Capell. 943-4218," I answered.

After about ten of the longest minutes of my life, he told me he'd contacted them and they were on their way.

I sat in the back room, wanting to look out to see if Uncle Jimmy or Aunt Margaret was there yet, but afraid I'd get in trouble if I peeked out the door. So I just sat there and waited.

And waited.

When Uncle Jimmy got there, I let out a sigh of relief. The police officer smiled at my uncle and said, "Well, I guess I don't have to ask who *you* are. This is the first time I've seen her smile since she got here."

Uncle Jimmy took me to his house. I drank some water and calmed down. When Mom and Dad got home a few hours later they took me home.

They all still tease me about it more than forty years later. Probably will for the rest of my life.

18

Where Did I Go?

Alice Klies

M y husband stood at the mirror, trimming the hair that grows in cavities as a man grows older. I stood next to him, trying to make my hair look fuller by teasing it with a three-prong comb.

He glanced at me and said, "You know, honey, it takes me longer to trim the hair in my nose and ears than it takes the barber to trim the hair on my head."

We started to laugh, and it took me a good fifteen minutes before I pulled myself together.

"Yes, I was just thinking that I wished for long hair . . . but I'm really just longing for hair, period!" I said.

By this time, I was sure I would end up on the floor because I laughed with such gulping and hiccupping that I folded my arms around my stomach, which led me to sit precariously on the edge of my vanity chair.

When I got myself under control, I took a long look in the mirror. I turned from side to side. I pulled at the roll at my waist and wondered if I should put on one of the slimming undergarments I'd bought weeks earlier.

My thoughts turned to a conversation with one of my much

younger girlfriends while having coffee the previous week. I had complained about weight gain and wrinkles when she said, "You look great. You should be counting your blessings."

When I looked at her, I thought, *Oh yeah, you should talk.* Her face doesn't look like a lined, wrinkled piece of thin fabric that was left in the clothes dryer too long. Her saucy, wavy hair swings perkily from side to side while I worry about whether I should have worn a hairpiece or a wig. She can push a cart with normal speed through grocery aisles. I clean off the cart handle with a sanitary wipe and then lean on the handle in order to stabilize my aching hip.

I know many articles are written about bodies and aging. I must admit I feel a little depressed when I hear or read them. Thank goodness my depression doesn't last long because much of the time, minutes afterward I can't remember if I've said it, read it, heard it, or even thought it.

I don't like that I snap and crack in the morning before I get to the kitchen to pull out a box of cereal that is supposed to do the snapping, crackling, and popping when I put milk on it.

Is it just me, or do all women over seventy have trouble trimming their toenails? Since my midsection isn't what it used to be and has broadened all the way to the edges of my hips — uniformity, so to speak — I find that when I bend, I can just about reach my knees. Too bad my feet aren't where my knees are.

I try to convince myself that my slightly larger curves are something I should embrace.

As a young adult, I felt the need to compete with the models on magazine covers, wanting to look like the girl wearing wings in a Victoria's Secret fashion show. I did all the things I knew were not healthy. I starved myself. I ran for miles each day. I took dangerous diet pills and laxatives.

I'm lucky to have no ill effects from those.

Maybe the time comes when we learn to accept our flaws.

Maybe.

Except last week when I met the super-granny who still bikes ten miles a day and weighs one hundred-twenty pounds. I came home, pressed my face against the mirror, turned and grimaced at my backside, and experienced a pang of wistfulness.

I walked away, then laughed out loud.

I've lost the old physical version of myself and moments of years past but I've I resigned myself to accepting the me of today: the rolls around my waist, the sagging jaw line, squiggles around my eyes, and the slow motor in my get up and go.

I accept them because I know my family and friends love me just the way I am. Most of all, I know God doesn't shake a finger at me. He loves me whether I am purple or pink, chucky or slim, disabled or active.

The one truly golden moment in my golden age of mature hips and wrinkles is the gold crown on a tooth that my dentist replaced recently with porcelain.

I sold that gold.

It gave me enough cash for a trip to Dairy Queen.

Do I lament those lost years or worry about my now ample curves and wrinkles?

Nah! That younger self still lives inside this older body . . . and enthusiastically enjoys an occasional ice cream sundae.

~ 19 ~

The God of New Beginnings

Norma C. Mezoe

Robert had an abusive childhood and endured multiple beatings from his stepfather. When he was a teen, he left his home and hitchhiked to another state where a family befriended him. While he was there, he dated Mary, one of the daughters.

Robert enlisted in the service and was gone for some time. When he went "home" on leave, he learned that Mary had married. Devastated, he returned to duty with a broken heart.

Eventually Robert married, but instead of contributing positively to his marriage, he dwelt on what might have been if he'd married his first love.

Fifty years later Robert still yearned for the girl who got away. At night after he went to bed, he carried on one-sided conversations with his former girlfriend. Although she wasn't present, he talked as though she were there.

Robert was unaware his wife heard these "conversations," which became intimate at times. When she confronted him, Robert denied having the one-way conversations with his former girlfriend. Yet they continued for eight years while Robert's communication with his wife became limited and was often laced with his angry words.

By choosing to live in the past instead of focusing on his present life, Robert — and his wife — lost the blessing God intended for their marriage.

If we are holding on to things of the past, things that can never be ours — as Robert was — God will help us let go and will give us a new beginning. But we must be willing, and we must ask.

20

Finding My Father

Sue Schlesman

I am sure that I had learned to say "Daddy" before I was two years old, but I don't remember ever saying it. I don't remember hearing my dad's voice or feeling what it was like for him to hold me. I don't remember any connection to him at all.

Without the pictures I have of him, I would have no recollection of what he even looked like because I have only one memory of him. I was sitting on my brother and cheering. Under my two-year-old legs, my brother was straddling a dark fuzzy form who was laughing and tickling us, I think. I can't recall his face or voice, but I'm sure it was him.

I asked my mom about it once, and she said my father often wrestled with us kids that way, piling on the living floor after dinner. I'm sure I would not remember this moment at all, except that it is my only living memory of my dad. Less than four months after my second birthday, my father was killed tragically in a Naval air-training mission. He was just thirty-three years old.

As I grew up, I always wondered about him — what he was like and if I were like him. After peppering relatives with carefully-timed questions, I learned bits of information that I pieced together like a patchwork quilt until I had created myself a version of my father, the family hero and the love of Mom's life.

Information was difficult to acquire because nobody talked about him very much. When I heard stories, they were told a few sentences at a time and cut off because they were accompanied by tears or quavering voices. I knew people wanted to talk about him and that their memories were precious and painful, so I carefully accumulated the facts over time. He had been an Eagle Scout, a pilot, a university professor, a printer, a musician, an artist, a naval aviator. He put himself through college by living at home, commuting, and joining the ROTC program. It took him six years, but he met my mother and convinced her to fall for him.

He cruised in the Mediterranean and the Pacific on subs and aircraft carriers. Twice, using the constellations, he navigated successfully back to the aircraft carrier when his plane's navigation equipment failed. He brought back pearls from Japan, lace from Italy, and wooden bowls from Hawaii.

I knew of him, but I did not know him. I mostly only understood that my mother loved and missed him, and that he had died tragically in the service of his country. Something about faulty instruments and a heavy storm in the California mountains.

It turns out, knowledge isn't enough to know someone. Even when relatives told me that he'd be proud of me or that he was looking down on me, I wasn't consoled. Who wants a father who just watches them from the sky? I wanted a father who was *present.*

When I was a little girl, I dreamed that a knock would sound at the front door, we would open it, and a tall, handsome Navy officer in his crisp, white uniform would be standing there.

He would say, "I didn't really die. There was an accident. I had amnesia, and I've just remembered who I was. I've been searching for you." Sometimes in my dreams he would lift me up in a big Hollywood embrace; most of the time, he would run to my mother and wrap his arms around her, and I would get to see them together — I would see my mother complete again and truly happy. The dream played through my mind like a movie.

We had no pictures of my dad displayed at our house. Some boxes in the attic held his things, and his footlocker contained his hats, uniforms, personal items, and the flag that had been draped over his coffin.

I understood I was not supposed to snoop inside the footlocker. It was the Holy of Holies in our house. I thought if I peeked inside, I'd probably drop dead and have to be dragged out of the attic by a string. Yet I did peek a couple times, and kept that secret hidden, tucked inside my heart with all the other secrets and unanswered questions about who my dad was and what had happened to him.

But grief has a determined way of making itself known. Of demanding answers. Resolution.

About forty years after my father died, my mother, brother, and I took a trip to visit my dad's older brother. While we were there, my cousin slipped me a scrapbook and said my uncle wanted me to have it. It contained photographs of my dad, newspaper clippings about the accident, his obituaries, memorabilia, and the actual death telegram from the Navy.

I read the articles about the crash and learned the names of the places and people involved. In doing so, I discovered that my brother and I belonged to a larger family whose members grieved together, even while they grieved separately. The crash had widowed seven women and left twenty-nine children fatherless. My parents were the youngest of the couples.

According to articles in the scrapbook, my father's plane was a large reconnaissance aircraft, the Lockheed SP-50 Neptune. I did a little Internet research and found mention on blogs and military websites of a few crashes. Eventually I found a detailed description of a naval crash on February 11, 1969 in the Santa Ana Mountains of southern California. My dad's crash.

Someone knew and cared enough to write about it.

I felt overwhelmed and overjoyed. With a click of the mouse, I found live footage from an ABC affiliate in southern California from 2008: I saw people walking across a debris-cluttered ridge, talking about their father's crash. I recognized their last name from the many articles in the scrapbook — they were touring their father's crash site. *My* father's crash site. Our fathers had been crewmembers together on the Neptune.

The on-screen journalist was interviewing an aviation archeologist who knew nearly everything about the crash.

I immediately found the archeologist's website and sent him an email, telling him who I was and asking if I could come see him. He responded the next day, thanking me for my dad's sacrifice and offering to lead me on a hike into the canyon. His empathy validated and comforted my unspoken sorrow.

Within two months, I was hiking the crash site with the archeologist's team. The aviation archeologist himself was moved to tears when he talked about the crash and the young men who had lost their lives. He had done impressive research: the official Navy report, photographs by himself and others, an interview with the air traffic controller. He had personally hiked the crash site several times. A local teenager in 1969, he had witnessed the explosion from his own front yard.

My dad had belonged to a squadron from Minneapolis/St. Paul. On a two-week drill, the crew had taken off from El Toro Air Force Base, near Mission Viejo, to practice nighttime touch-and-go's in the desert terrain of the Santa Ana Mountains.

It was raining.

After a few minutes in the air, the sky assaulted the aircraft with torrents of rain and gusts of high wind not uncommon for the area; it was recorded as the worst weather of the year. Radio transmission was sketchy. Whether the mistake occurred in the cockpit or at air traffic control, faulty coordinates send the Neptune flying into Harding Canyon at a speed of one hundred-fifty miles per hour and an altitude of three thousand feet.

The Saddleback peaks surrounding them rose to five thousand eight hundred feet.

As the plane entered Modeskja Canyon, something — maybe lightning — must have alerted the crew to the close, surrounding mountains. They had no room to clear the peaks. The crew sent out a "mayday" and plunged straight into the first ridge. The impact caused the engines to explode, and the crew died instantly. The wings were torn off and the plane continued breaking apart as it careened into the next ridge. Large pieces of the plane imbedded themselves into the mountainsides; shrapnel and debris hurtled across three ridges and valleys and settled into the dense chaparral.

When we arrived at the mountaintop, I could see the Air Force base in the distance. I climbed down to the impact zone with an American flag and thought of how it might feel to realize death is milliseconds away. I descended into the canyon, handling, almost caressing, pieces of the plane that I found along the way, thinking of my father and wondering if he'd touched them forty years ago. This had been his plane. His final moments had happened here.

A solitary crewmember's seat lay at the bottom of the canyon, completely intact, as if waiting for its passenger. I sat in it and said a prayer and read a little speech about my dad's life. I placed a memorial there to honor his sacrifice.

Peace seemed to settle over the debris around me.

I breathed deeply, feeling this place where he had lost his life. Feeling him and knowing him.

I realized that whether I'm searching to know my earthly father, or struggling to understand my heavenly Father, knowing begins with an acceptance of his character and love. My relationship with my biological father requires an understanding of his purpose and duty, of his decision to place himself in harm's way. This understanding culminates with honoring the sacrifice he made.

Sitting in Modjeska Canyon and standing at the impact zone were holy, footlocker moments for me. I felt a spiritual connection and a closeness to both my father and God that I could not have anticipated.

It felt as though Grief had opened the front door of his house, let me venture back out into the world, and then he shut himself back inside, alone.

And God whispered to me, as He did throughout other memorial moments in Scripture. He named Himself, so I would understand Him better and connect to Him more fully, *I am here. I am Jehovah-Shammah, the God who is present.*

Death could not keep me from a love relationship with my Heavenly Father or from one with my earthly father. Only Grief could do that.

21

Yalem

Laura Sweeney

I'm scratching out a poem from the line "a woman on the brink" when Yalem calls. It has been four years since I last heard from my friend and mentor — the spring before I moved to southern Illinois for my MFA. Her timing has often been uncanny.

"Your timing is excellent," I laugh. "I'm about to defend my poetry manuscript later this week." It has been eight years almost to the day since my first master's defense. Afterward we had sat on the patio of Stomping Grounds sipping white wine.

"How's Academia?" I ask now, knowing full well the fortress . . . those on the inside want out, those on the outside want in.

"They're squeezing the sweat and blood — every last drop — from fewer and fewer faculty," she replies. "Never seen it so ugly."

Things hadn't worked out on the coast as planned for Yalem and her husband. Despite their retirement plans out east, they had moved back to the Midwest.

"He's tired," she says of her husband and his career as an agricultural economics professor, now department chair. "All he wants is to ride his bike, maybe be a postman."

She laughs.

It's so good to hear Yalem's soft voice.

An Ethiopian refugee who fled unrest in her country and became a fierce women's rights advocate in the States, in times past she might have shared her own hardships.

She's a model of a non-traditional student who let nothing stop her dedication to higher education, although she has confessed she could not have climbed the ranks without her husband's privilege.

I've admired her persistence to earn her PhD by the time she was fifty, and appreciated her encouragement for me to earn my PhD despite being middle-aged.

"I'm not teaching Gender and Sexuality in this climate," she tells me. "I've been promoted to Professor of Practice. Just my online Women in International Perspective class."

"I didn't get into Nebraska," I tell her, the ping of lagging behind stinging. "I got into a human rights program at Binghamton, but . . . no funding."

Moving sideways in a zigzag seems to have become my norm.

"No money," she repeats in that academic way of knowing.

Neither of us had thought it would be so difficult for me to advance.

"I thought you were here." She sighs and explains how she had driven to Ames for an emergency dental appointment. "It's deserted; everything's shut down."

"Sounds creepy," I say, then ask about our favorite coffee shop.

"Closed. And finding an open hotel was tricky."

I miss our coffee chats. I'd arrive at Stomping Grounds a few minutes early. To pass the time while I waited for Yalem, I'd pick up a copy of *Whistling Shade* from the newsstand, scan the business cards displayed on the shelf, consider the artist statements posted on the wall, glance at the bulletin board, think about attending a lecture.

I miss our corner table and how we'd share a hummus and baba platter but instead of baba, we'd substitute olive tapenade. I miss their crepes — banana Nutella, berry mascarpone, crepe monsieur. I miss how she'd pray over our lunch — her Greek salad, my egg salad on multigrain toast.

I'm tired, tired, tired of the pandemic cuisine . . . and isolation.

"I'm graduating into another crisis," I vent. I want to tell her I feel like giving up, that I may never advance beyond the master's level, may never take hold of the words she said so long ago: "There is something so professorial about you."

"You will get your break," Yalem assures me now. "This just adds texture."

Texture. I recall her beautiful scarves. How elegantly she'd tied them! How scruffy I'd felt in my sweatshirts. I don't know how to tie a scarf like she does. There's beauty in the way she arranges them, a knowledge of the drape. At a conference at University of Illinois she'd hung her scarves in our hotel room and told me, "These are my jewels."

Here, in the current scuffle to survive the shifting sands of Academia and a pandemic I feel I've lost all sophistication. I feel forever underemployed.

"When do things get better?" I lament.

"At least the decisions are yours," my mentor encourages me. "You don't have to follow someone else's career. You can apply to other institutions. Maybe Canada."

Perhaps, but as a single woman I know what the possibilities are while the world is in lockdown.

At women's studies forums, Yalem and I had indulged in abundant spreads of sandwiches and salads, cakes and crisps. Afterward we'd walked across campus to her mustard-colored-brick house.

There were no travel bans. I watered her garden when she and her husband vacationed in Belgium, were on sabbatical in Australia, or led service trips in Ethiopia. When they returned, she and I would sit on their deck and eat decadent European-dark-chocolate while she showed me photos. The economy was stagnant then, but nowhere near this crisis.

We have volumes to chat about now, but we don't talk long. "Just remember: This too shall pass," she says, ending our phone call.

How I miss my friend and mentor! I miss our marathon chats, our post-coffee-shop walks to her home, sharing chocolate on her terrace while we finished those chats.

I miss the texture, the stability Yalem's reassurances brought to my life. Through her, I experienced Proverbs 27:17 (NIV): *As iron sharpens iron, so one person sharpens another.*

Oh, to have one of her beautiful scarves to serve as a visual reminder of Yalem.

Maybe then I would not feel quite so lost. So alone.

22

On the Backside
of the Boondocks

Vicki H. Moss

One summer, during a period of my life when I began to hear from God in the most amazing ways — ways that sometimes scared my socks off because previously I hadn't been used to hearing from Him so clearly — I was driving by myself down I-65 through Alabama to Destin, Florida. My goal was meeting up with my daughter, a friend of hers, and the friend's parents at their beach home.

The plan was to do some bicycling, have lots of reading time while resting beneath an umbrella, maybe jump a wave or two, eat lots of seafood, watch great movies at night, and relax in general while having fun.

While listening to a Christian radio program just north of Montgomery, Alabama I was inspired to pray: "Lord, what would you have me do?"

While I was praying — with my eyes open of course — I saw a sign on the right side of the road that notified travelers of a Confederate Memorial Park up ahead. I felt a strong tug on the heartstrings, or in my spirit — what was happening was questionable — to go there. I said, "Well, that's great, Lord, but you know I'm expected in Destin. The beach and a book are calling, and I don't have time to go sight-seeing today."

Yet the strong feeling to go to the park wouldn't dissipate. So I said, "What am I supposed to do there? Can't I visit another time when I'm not on a tight schedule?"

Though I heard nothing audibly, I somehow sensed the answer was a firm, clear "no." The exit ramp loomed ahead and at the last possible moment, I found myself swerving off the interstate to head toward the park. "Okay," I said at the stop sign, "I'll go. But this had better be you, Lord, and would you please tell me what I'm supposed to be doing there? I know I'm a Civil War history buff, but this is not the time to study history. And I really don't have time to traipse through the woods looking at cannons and cannon balls. I'm supposed to be dining on crab boil tonight and I don't want to miss that supper!"

From the interstate, it seemed like I drove forever, the tires lapping up mile after mile. Once, thinking I'd lost my ever lovin' mind, I thought I would turn around; but the urgency was still there and I couldn't bring myself to do it, so I kept driving.

At last I saw the turn that would supposedly lead me to the park and my destination. Or, perhaps, destiny? Or, God forbid, a lurking pervert with a knife or gun. Maybe both.

Where on earth was I? I was on the backside of the boondocks in a heartache-of-a-looking place in who-knows-where Alabama.

I prayed I wouldn't have a flat tire because my AAA membership had expired and I didn't know a soul to call if I had car trouble in this God-forsaken portion of the state.

I began to sense that God was sending me to talk with

someone. Yikes! Witnessing to others made me extremely nervous because I had been taught from a young age to never talk about religion or politics.

"Are you kidding me?" I objected. "You're sending me into the boonies to talk to someone about Jesus and the Gospel? Don't you have the wrong person for this job? Where's a preacher when you need one?"

I turned up the air conditioner because I felt a heat wave coming on. I took a deep breath and tried to calm myself because all of my old arguments were rising to the surface.

"Okay," I finally agreed. "I'll try. But you have to help me. You *know* I'm not good at this. No knives. No dodging bullets. *Nothing* scary. And no rabid dogs!"

Not long afterward I spotted a small church. When I saw the next turn I drove down the other road and was finally in the park. As I eased up to a small museum, I noticed only one other automobile in the parking lot. Good. Just the one person I was supposed to speak with. I let out a sigh of relief.

Until I saw *them*.

Terrified, I sucked in my breath. There, over on the other side of the parking lot, was an entire family eating lunch at some picnic tables. But this wasn't just any family picnic. It was a family reunion! They even had a name banner: HUNTINGDON! Holy cow! Their cars were parked on the other side of the museum parking lot. And there were scads of them.

My stomach was queasy now. I thought I'd lose the Cheetos I'd just eaten. I sat in my car and fought the urge to tremble. "Lord, if this is a joke, it's not funny. I am *not* going over there. Those people will have me committed.

"And what would you have me say? 'Oh, hello there. The Lord took me off the interstate several miles and half-a-tank-of-gas-ago to tell you that Jesus is King of kings and Lord of lords and Hallelujah, praise be to God, everybody here needs to be SAVED!' Sorry to be sarcastic Lord, but they will have me institutionalized as sure as the world turns. I'm *not* going over there. I just *can't*."

Hand wringing and ring twisting commenced. "Being a Christian is too *hard*!"

I looked at my watch and tried to calm down. I was going to be late. The pressing-in-feeling that I was to speak with someone about Jesus wouldn't go away. There was someone in that park I was supposed to speak with. "Okay. Look, Lord. I can't do it. I'm going to calm down, go in that tiny building of a museum, and, since I'm here, look around. Maybe the person is in *there*. Exhorting to hordes is out of my league."

When I entered the museum, there was one person sitting behind the desk and we simultaneously said, "Hello." But then a man and his son stepped through the door behind me. Now there were three people. Who was I supposed to say something to? And what was I supposed to say? "You know God, it would really help if you would fill me in on *the plan*. Which person? What words? I'm sweating more than Civil War bullets here. Help a girl out." Nothing. I was hearing absolutely nothing. I looked at my watch. Time was a-wastin' and so were the waves.

But then, as always, my curiosity got the better of me. I took in many of the displays. The Confederate Memorial Park wasn't just any Civil War park. This place seemed to be more than a museum. It was a "moving tribute to the men and boys who took up arms in defense of their home state during the Civil War." I discovered that there was also an Old Soldiers' Home for Confederate Veterans on the site, and the one-hundred-two-acre park included not only the museum, but a research facility, historic structures, ruins and two cemeteries containing over three hundred Confederate soldiers. From 1902 to 1939 the complex had grown to include twenty-two buildings, in addition to the residents. There had been a hospital, administration building, mess hall, a dairy barn, and more. I was hooked.

Ninety-one Confederate veterans and nineteen widows of the veterans had lived on this land during its heyday. As the population dwindled, the two cemeteries were filled. It was estimated that as many as eight hundred residents had lived at the site over the years. The last surviving veteran living at the home died in 1934. The complex was closed in 1939 and five of the veterans' widows were moved to a facility in Montgomery.

There was so much information in this tiny museum. I found myself soaking in the history, though I was still anxious about whom I was supposed to speak with. Then the man and his son left. Good. Two down. One to go. Perhaps I was supposed to speak with the museum attendant at the desk.

This was all so *questionable*.

Still doubtful, I said, "Okay, Lord, if you're behind this, I'll do it. I'll go chitchat with the attendant and if, in conversation, she says the word . . . what word? I wracked my brain. Then a thought of the little church on the highway before turning onto the park's road popped into my head. *Church!* Yes! If she says the word *church*, I'll witness to her if you'll tell me what you want me to say."

Quaking in my sandals I approached the woman, then, had second thoughts. *What if she isn't friendly? Stop it. She works in a museum. It's her job to be friendly. Just go talk with her and get to the bottom of this detour.*

As we began to talk, the attendant answered my questions about the grounds and Civil War tidbits. We had a great chat. Peace fell over me and I enjoyed our conversation. She seemed grateful to be talking with another human being. And I was so grateful to be released from testifying at the Hungtingdon Reunion, I'd totally forgotten I was supposed to *speak* with someone. Then, out of the blue the woman mentioned the word *church*! I felt like I'd been jolted with a low voltage cattle prod. She'd just said there was a *church* in the park. *That's odd in itself. Okay. I'm on point like a bird dog, Lord. Now what?* But I wasn't being downloaded any information.

Then she mentioned *church* again!

I winged it. "You know, I noticed that before I got to the park, there was also a little church before the park entrance road."

Then she began to open up like a lotus blossom about her personal life. "Yes, there are a lot of little churches around here. Why I quit going. People can't get along so churches keep splitting and before you know it there's a new church that's cropped up. I need to get back into church, though. I miss it."

A flash of subtle sorrow passed over her beautiful face.

Ahhhhhh. There was my cue. And suddenly, I knew what I was supposed to tell her. "You know, nowadays, you can go online and download Bible studies from the internet." And then the message was so easy-peasy after that. I shared with her about several different Bible studies I'd taught women at my church.

Her face lit up the entire room as I shared more, especially about some of the wonderful God-moments I'd had.

Now she was hooked. "I hadn't thought of ordering a Bible study over the internet!" she said. "I'll check into those studies right away!"

"I'll be praying for you to find a new church and until then, I think you'll enjoy the studies I've suggested. Thanks so much for sharing your knowledge on the Civil War. I hope to come back when I have more time to explore." We said our goodbyes. And the urgency to give someone a message was gone.

This woman was definitely *the one*. As I settled in behind the steering wheel of my car, I could see that the Huntingdon's were still enjoying barbeque and watermelon. And I thanked the Lord I didn't feel the slightest urge to go over there and "exhort."

But back on the road headed for I-65 and the crab boil, I had another "word" with God. "Lord, why didn't you have someone from the Huntingdon family reunion go speak with this woman? Or someone from one of the many churches around here? Or that man with his son? I could have been waylaid by bandits and cutthroats this far out. Why would you have me leave the interstate and drive all this way . . . why *me?*"

Immediately I heard in my spirit, "Because of your passion for Civil War history and your passion for *me*."

Oh, *now* the Lord was talking.

Wow. Just wow.

And then I asked, "Then why couldn't you give me a hint about what I was supposed to be doing. Some clues! *Something.* I felt hung out to dry! I need strategic sandboxes if I'm going to be desert fighting. Battle plans. I need to know where to place my bazookas. You know I almost had a heart attack when I saw that family reunion going on. I could have had more help there — don't you think?"

And though I didn't want to hear it, what I heard next in my spirit made sense. "Faith." Evidently I didn't have enough. And He planned on building mine through trials.

Then several other words began to flood into my spirit. *Obedience. Trust. Testing.*

"Okay, I get it. Guess I got a D+ on that test. But thanks anyway for giving me the right words at the last minute. And I know you've allowed others to have even more difficult moments than I had back there. At least I didn't have the Red Sea in front of me and the Egyptian army breathing down my back. I really would have had a heart attack — you know deep water scares me. But one more thing, can I at least have a storm at sea while I'm in Destin? You know — one of those brilliant electrical storms that never comes inland to do damage but is such a spectacular show?"

Nothing. No more words of wisdom. Simply nothing. Why were all of my conversations with Him mostly one-sided? Sigh. I turned the Christian radio station back on and kept my hood ornament pointed south.

When I arrived, the crab boil was just getting started. I hadn't missed a thing. The beach and bicycling could wait until tomorrow.

Over buttered corn on the cob, sea fare, and crab-pot boiled potatoes, I was asked if I'd encountered a lot of traffic on the way down." I hesitantly replied, "Well, you wouldn't believe what happened right before Montgomery . . . ."

"Traffic jam?"

Then I thought better of sharing something so personal and

beautifully scripted by God. No one would believe what happened to me; only those who had totally free-fallen in abandonment for Christ and had experienced strange and questionable things too. I was like Mary in a sense, a girl who "kept all these things, and pondered them in her heart" (Luke 2:19). I simply wanted to bask in His presence. I even feared "what man would say." So I veered toward safety until I could process the experience more fully. Alone.

I was in a jam alright. Let's just say it was bumper-to-bumper hair-raising with a major bullet-dodging-detour.

I smiled. "It wasn't all *that* bad." And it struck me that no backside of the boondocks is ever God-forsaken.

~ 23 ~

Tarantula Lost!

Theresa Cates

Often, when a child goes to college, or is otherwise absent from home, Mom is called on to care for things left behind.

Such was the case when my son left for his freshman year of college. He had always kept an assortment of "critters" ranging from geckos and salamanders to rhinoceros beetles and Madagascar hissing roaches, and more. (I thanked God sincerely when those roaches died for lack of something in their diet, because I was ready to contract with an insect hit man to take them out!)

So, it fell to this Mama to take care of the tarantula he had received on his 16th birthday. Now, several years later, it still occupied an aquarium in his downstairs bedroom. Every week or so, I would purchase crickets at the local pet shop to feed it. It "gave me the willies" to see it pounce on the unlucky crickets. In my head, I knew the tarantula was pretty harmless (they can bite but it is no worse than a wasp sting) but still . . . the thing creeped me out. I dreamed of its demise and my vocational change from caretaker to pallbearer!

Then, one day when I went downstairs to feed it, the aquarium was empty! The hairy thing was loose and I had no idea where it lurked! Visions of it pouncing on my head from a dark corner filled my mind. I ran upstairs, grabbed the broom, and returned to the room to see if I could find the errant creature.

Armed with my broom, I slowly scanned the room, carefully peering into every nook and cranny as best I could while standing in the center of the room trying to distance myself from perches from which it could launch itself at me. Finally, I spied something unusual on top of my son's desk. It was a curled up, shiveled up mass. I poked it with the end of the broomstick. It didn't move. Guilty joy bubbled up in a giggle . . . the tarantula was dead!

Gleefully, I phoned my son. Trying to sound somber I said, "Honey, I have bad news. Your tarantula died." And then I proceeded to tell him what happened.

"Mom," he said, "describe to me what you see." So, I described the dried-up remains of his long-cherished pet.

He chuckled, "It's not dead, Mom. It shed its exoskeleton!"

"What! You've got to be kidding!" I wasn't expecting that answer. I was prepared to mourn his loss with him . . . joyfully!

The thought of that creeping, eight-legged arachnid being loose in my house with a new — "bigger and badder" — lease on life filled me with dread! Now I again had to wonder when it would jump out at me when I least expected it.

As I contemplated this possibility, it occurred to me I should find out how long tarantulas can live. The answer didn't bring any comfort. Their life span varies from seven to twenty-five years.

In my mind, long years of anxiously searching dark corners of my house stretched out before me. I berated myself for ever having indulged my son's obsession with "creepy crawlers." I was now suffering the consequences of that indulgence.

What had I been thinking?!

From that day forward, always vigilant for my eight-legged nemesis, I never went downstairs without being armed with my trusty broom, ready to swat that creeping arachnid should it show its beady-eyed face.

I didn't even divulge its escape to my girlfriends for fear they would refuse to enter my house.

I kept an ever-watchful eye for its presence, but time and necessity have a way of making us comfortable with the uncomfortable.

Several months later, I headed downstairs to do laundry. Carrying a laundry basket full of clothes down stairs doesn't allow for the carrying of a broom. I had left the broom on the porch the day before, anyway.

That is how I had ended up downstairs without my weapon.

After I had loaded the washing machine and had turned to head back up the stairs, I spied a dark object the size of a baseball creeping across the carpet in the adjoining room. It was the tarantula! It still lived after all this time. I had hoped it had succumbed to natural causes.

I didn't have the broom to smash it. What could I do?

I grabbed an empty mason jar with a lid off of the shelf in the laundry room and worked up the courage to approach the now-alerted tarantula. Better to end this now than let it get away and have to continue this game of hide and seek. Somehow — it is a blur to me now — I scooped it up in the glass jar and slammed down the lid. Victory at long last was mine! I returned it to the aquarium, assured myself the lid was on properly and went out to buy crickets for the wretched creature.

When my son left college and joined the Marine Corp, I

continued to care for that tarantula. I took care of that thing until he married a beautiful Marine and I demanded they take it with them to their new home.

My watch was finally over.

I understand the tarantula lived a number of years more. It fell to my daughter-in-law to care for it while my son was deployed overseas.

It could have died from natural causes . . . but I wonder?

She is an excellent marksman.

~ 24 ~

Lost Moments Recovered

Leigh-Anne Burley

I trapped childhood memories in a complex maze of forgotten moments of people, places, and events woven into a barren landscape. By age fourteen, I knew something was wrong, but I didn't know what, or how to fix it. It felt like a madman had messed with the wiring in my brain.

Dissociative Identity Disorder (DID) is a mental condition characterized by two or more different personality states, distinct behavior, memory, and cognition in one individual. I had numerous personalities from sustained early childhood abuse. At first, I was treated for anxiety and depression and placed on medication, which didn't ease my symptoms. An accurate diagnosis of DID arrived years later, and I was treated primarily by working through repressed traumatic moments.

Treatment involved finding my core in a convoluted vortex where "up" seemed "down," similar to walking on the ceiling. Recovery lasted a decade, allowing painful memories to surface. These were hard years for my family and me to endure. I felt odd and undoubtedly different, so I didn't let anyone close for fear of rejection and abandonment. I'd had plenty of that in my life.

I am grateful to my family and a few friends for their

support, but they could only take me so far, as my trust level was virtually non-existent.

The lasting and essential help came through the steadfast presence of Jesus, embracing my deep sorrow and anger. His abiding love in His written Word revealed His character of tender mercy and grace. For the first time, I thought I might be loveable. I had a long way to go to understand that I wasn't the nonperson at my pulverized center, as the many voices in my head said.

I didn't know who I was. Too many altars competed for my time, convincing me "*this* is who I am." The background noise was like a radio scanning different stations; but this was flipping through the gamut of emotions — fearful, angry, sad, nervous, and sometimes weird and funny — all without my control. I was desperate and sinking. I wanted to live, but I wanted a way out if this was my life. I had to find higher, solid ground to safety. I couldn't climb out. I needed a rescuer to grab and pull me out of this quicksand pit of hell.

When I hid in the back of a closet like a frightened child,
He crawled in and found me.
When I could not stand,
He knelt, held, and rocked me like a tender mother.
When I couldn't go on breathing,
He breathed for me.
When I lost my mind,
He held my spirit.
When I tumbled into darkness,
He firmly grasped my hand.
Jesus is everything to me.
He completely identified with my suffering.

He turned my mourning into joy.
The rough terrain that was once ashes is now beautiful.
Nothing is impossible with God.
All glory is His.

Before the foundations of the world, God, in His infinite wisdom, formed and fashioned me for His good purposes to live with Him, Christ-centered for all eternity.

I am His beloved child, and He is my dear Father.

~ 25 ~

Saying Goodbye

Lola Di Giulio De Maci

I never met my paternal grandmother, my father's mother. We lived an ocean apart. It was that same ocean my father sailed across when he left his homeland of Italy and ventured to a new land called America. He dreamed of a better life for himself and the family he would one day have. And he believed this new country could help fulfill those dreams. He was seventeen years old.

His older brother had already made the journey to America and waited anxiously to welcome the brother he had played with in the hills above Rome. They had been an inseparable twosome, climbing fruit trees or running through tall grasses, and helping their parents till the soil in the surrounding fields.

Their younger brother joined them in their adopted homeland years after my fther arrived.

As time and life unfolded, neither my father nor his brothers ever saw their mother again. My father wept freely when he received the news that his mother had died. I cried too, feeling I had lost a part of me I would never know.

No one ever said what my grandmother died of. I don't think anyone actually knew. They were told she had just quietly slipped away one morning.

I have often wondered if she died of a broken heart.

It must have been hard for her to say good-bye to her sons. I'm sure she realized that they left their boyhood home because they dreamed of a better life for themselves.

And I'm sure that she wished them a good life . . . all the while keeping each one locked safely in that part of her heart reserved as "For Mothers Only."

26

From Lost to Stranded

Diana Leagh Matthews

Every door kept closing in my face.

After graduating college, every door continued to close in my face. My dreams of graduate school did not pan out, my job ended, and I was lost and wondering. What next? Where do I go from here?

No matter how much I asked and begged the Lord for answers there were none. Everywhere I turned the doors continued to close.

Then I met a man and fell in love, thinking he was the man I'd been waiting for.

Early in our relationship, I began to question a few things he said and did. One afternoon, my insides were in knots. No matter what I did, I could not stop the gnawing within me.

I took a long drive through the country, before ending up at an old country church. I walked around the church praying and seeking answers. The gnawing continued to increase and grow stronger and stronger.

I prayed, "Lord, I'll do anything you want but please don't take this man from my life. I can't live without him."

I had no idea I'd prayed a prayer that would change my life for the worse.

Everything seemed to be working out when I found a job in the city where he lived and I moved to be closer to him.

What a mistake! For three years I was in a living hell and abusive relationship.

During this time the only place I could turn was to the Lord. I went from being lost to being stranded. I wondered if I would ever get out of this albatross of a relationship.

Eventually, I surrendered my relationship to the Lord and He removed me from it.

Only once I was out of the relationship did I begin to recognize the foothold the devil had on my life. He had taken a time of weakness and loss and used it to grab my attention. The Lord had tried to warn me, but I'd refused to listen and thought I knew best.

The Lord did answer my prayers, but nothing turned out the way I dreamed or imagined. The Lord knew best, but had to allow me to prove it to myself. Before that happened, things went from bad to worse to terrible to awful to unbearable over the course of three years.

We are told: *Be sober, be watchful: your adversary the devil, as a roaring lion, walketh about, seeking whom he may devour* (1 Peter 5:8 asv).

Do you feel lost? What areas of your life does the devil look to devour?

Who is your stronghold?

27

Never Too Late

Bob Blundell

I've learned two indisputable truths about our Maker. First, His love for us is unconditional, regardless of sins we've committed. Never is it more apparent than in the beautiful story of the Prodigal Son in Luke's gospel, that God the Father loves and forgives all, regardless of one's transgressions, or how lost they may seem to be. Second, it is never too late to seek Him and ask for redemption and forgiveness. Even when you believe you're not worthy.

This is a story of three men and their journeys toward becoming who God meant them to be. They were dramatically different. Yet their destinations were the same. But of more importance than the twists and turns of these men's lives, is the undeniable truth of God's everlasting love for us.

* * *

Bill became disillusioned with the Catholic faith while studying at the seminary when he was a teenager. As a child he had dreamed of entering the priesthood one day, but after several years, he became disgruntled with what he termed politics and theological disagreements within the church. In his confusion he abandoned his dream and turned his back on the Church and its teachings.

Bill is in his late sixties now, an academic who has spent his adult life as a college professor. Over time, he's constructed walls built on the resentment he experienced decades ago. Even after marrying a devout Catholic woman when he was in his 30s, the barriers he had carefully nurtured, grew stronger, and his disillusionment evolved into anger.

Three years ago, after encouragement from friends, Bill agreed to attend a men's weekend retreat sponsored by his wife's church. His interest was purely academic. He expected to revalidate the bitterness he felt toward Catholicism. For two days, he sat among the other retreatants, processing what he saw and heard. His wife prayed for him each day, but toward the end of the weekend he had become more convinced the decision he'd made forty years earlier was the right one.

Then something incredible happened. Bill can't explain his sudden transformation other than to say God suddenly opened his eyes to the truth, much like the Lord opened the minds of the disciples after His return recorded in the book of Luke. The walls Bill had reinforced over four decades crumbled and fell. For the first time since he was a child, he saw clarity and truth.

I had the privilege of being with Bill when the Holy Spirit came upon him, and I will always remember the light that filled his eyes when his hope was restored.

Bill is now an active, committed leader in his church. After many years of darkness, the beauty of his faith has been rekindled and is alive in his heart.

* * *

Lee was born in Beijing and spent his first twenty years living under a harsh communist regime. His parents were professors at universities in China in the 60s. As a small child, Lee witnessed public beatings and executions that were part of the government's attempt to suppress those who didn't follow Mao's teachings.

When he was six, Lee and his parents were imprisoned in a camp for dissidents. Each day his mother and father were forced to march through the camp gates to perform hard labor in the fields, leaving him alone in their tiny two-room cell. As he watched them being taken away each morning, Lee lived in fear that they might not return and he would be alone in the world.

At age twenty-one, Lee fled China with forty-two dollars in his pocket and a desperate desire to escape the oppression. Although he spoke little English, he found ways to provide for his education, eventually getting a PhD in Psychology at a university in the United States. But even as he achieved academic and professional success, he struggled with PTSD from the traumas he had been exposed to as a child.

For over two decades, Lee traveled the globe in desperate pursuit of the true meaning to his existence, and to replace the cloud of darkness that had followed him since China. His journey took him to distant lands as he explored over a dozen religions and cults. Hope began to flicker and fade until he succumbed to deep depression that almost drove him to take his life.

Lee told me he had been prepared to surrender to death, believing it would give him greater peace than he had received in this world. But after praying for an end to his darkness, late one evening he sat in front of his laptop, searching the Internet for the nearest Catholic church, one of the few Christian faiths he had not pursued.

On a church website, he saw a picture of Mary with her Son,

Jesus, cradled tenderly in her arms, and he suddenly knew he was being called. After a long trek across five continents, experiencing Christian and pagan cultures, Lee had finally come home.

In 2016 during Easter vigil, I walked in a procession next to Lee and eleven other new Christians who were baptized in the name of the Father, Son, and Holy Spirit. As he received the sacrament of baptism, Lee stood in the pale light of the chapel and wept tears of gratitude and relief. He had finally reached the end of his journey.

Socrates wrote, '"It is the unexamined life that is not worth living." My dear friend has indeed examined many facets of this incredible world the Lord has given us. Now, he has finally found what eluded him for so many years: peace and joy through God.

* * *

My path intersected with Jose's one night in the parking lot of a Christian retreat facility. Although we attended different churches and didn't know each other, we were paired together directing cars for church members attending a multi-denominational event. As we waited under the stars on a warm, humid evening, Jose shared his story with me.

He was born in Monterrey, Mexico, the son of devout Christian parents. His father died when he was a small boy, leaving Jose's mother to raise him and his three sisters. When he was ten, like many of the boys in his neighborhood, Jose joined a local gang. By the time he was fourteen, he had advanced in rank and made more money in two weeks than his mother earned in a year.

Jose led a harsh, dangerous life for many years and after being stabbed in a drug deal gone bad, he had fled to the United States when he was twenty-five. In Texas, a drug addict with an extensive criminal history and a penchant for violence, he again became involved with gangs and lived just one step ahead of the law and a violent demise.

His life was in shambles. He lived in fear of being killed by rival gang members or taken into custody by police. He had no money and was homeless, but afraid to seek shelter from friends in fear of being found.

One day, his cousin suggested Jose attend a church retreat.

Jose laughed. "My church days are long behind me."

But his cousin persisted. "What do you have to lose? You'll have a roof over your head for three nights, food to eat, and I'll pay your way."

Jose considered the offer. The idea of having a temporary refuge from perils waiting for him out in the world, appealed to him. He decided he had nothing to lose and accepted his cousin's generosity.

After two days, Jose grew restless and planned to leave the next morning and seek the familiar surroundings of the alleys he had called home for several weeks. After breakfast, he distanced himself from other participants and walked toward the entrance of the facility.

Then suddenly, something told him to stop.

"God spoke to me," Jose told me. "It was like a movie flashing through my mind. I could see everything I had done wrong in my life. All the people I had hurt. The lives I had destroyed and the crimes I had committed." He hesitated. "And I could see my poor mother sitting in our living room each day, praying for me. And then," he went on to say, "God told me everything would be okay."

In the glow from the streetlamp above us, tears glistened in his eyes, and I could feel the incredible power of that moment in Jose's life. I knew God's promise to love and take care of him would always be there for him.

Jose is married now and has a two-year-old son. He works as a mechanic. He and his family attend church each Sunday. Jose has also reunited with his mother, who faithfully waited for him all those volatile years, doing the only thing she could do . . . which was plead with the Lord for His blessing for her son.

* * *

Each of these men, their struggles distinctly different, had given up hope. They were convinced their sins were too damning, their lives too broken to aspire for something better. They felt too lost, so believed it was too late for them to find peace and joy with our Maker. But now they know, even in times of struggles and suffering, He will always be there. Waiting. Seeking. Finding.

More important than the twists and turns of these men's lives is the undeniable truth of God's everlasting love for us.

I myself will pasture My sheep . . . .
The lost I will search out, the strays I will bring back.

Ezekiel 34:11, 16 NASB

~ 28 ~

Right Place, Wrong Time

Diana C. Derringer

Humble yourselves, therefore, under God's mighty hand,
that he may lift you up in due time.

1 Peter 5:6 NIV

I packed our bags, prepared and practiced my workshop presentation, and checked that everything in the house was in order. We enjoyed our drive to the motel, unloaded the car, and stood in line to check in.

"I'm sorry. I don't see your name."

I spelled my name for the clerk, and she checked again. "We have you down for next weekend."

"You're kidding," I said. I told her I was with a group, so she checked other names on our list. Sure enough, all were listed for the following weekend. My mind began scrolling the challenges of correcting the motel's mistake.

Then the manager pulled the reservations contract, as I verified online conference information.

They were right. I was wrong.

So, we loaded the car again and drove home, embarrassed but a bit wiser.

I had checked and double-checked everything under my control. However, I failed to double-check the date established by the one in charge, and as a result we had wasted time and energy on a trip we would only have to make again a week later.

How often do we do that in our relationship with God? We see a need. We sense God's leadership, but then barrel ahead in our own power. We fail to consult the One in charge for divine direction and timing.

PRAYER: Omniscient God, forgive us for dragging our feet or running ahead of your perfect plan. Amen.

~ 29 ~

The Birthday, World Series, and Pumpkin Pie

Cecil Taylor

I try to blame the whole episode on the 1986 World Series, but no one lets me get away with that excuse.

In October 1986, shortly after our first anniversary, I decided to surprise my diabetic wife, Sara, with a sugar-free pumpkin pie for her birthday. A shaky cook at best, I had never made the recipe before, but it was in her new diabetic cookbook, so what could go wrong?

Sara was a professional singer. While she was at a rehearsal, I made a pumpkin pie.

There are two points of view about what happened. Let me shift to Sara's side of the story before explaining my story of being left alone in the kitchen.

I had already gone to sleep by the time she returned from rehearsal, so Sara crawled into bed, stirring me. "I saw a pumpkin pie in the kitchen!"

Me: "Yes. And it's sugar free, too."

Sara: "Aw, that's sweet! And the kitchen is perfectly clean!"

Me: "Yes, and it got messy after you left, what with having

to clean up the pans and blender from boiling the eggs for the pie and all."

Sara, slowly: "Why did you boil eggs?"

Me, even more slowly, sensing I had done something wrong: "I'm not going to tell you."

Sara pleaded for me to tell her what happened, finally applying one of the biggest lies she ever said to me: "I promise I won't tell anyone!"

So, my tale of baking the pumpkin pie unfolded.

Sara must have laughed for five minutes straight before she could speak again.

Here's what happened. You must understand that while I was making the pumpkin pie, I was also watching one of the most gripping games in World Series history — a game between the Boston Red Sox and the New York Mets. Baseball fans will understand my divided attention when I explain this was the Buckner game. (Like me, Red Sox first baseman Bill Buckner experienced an infamous evening, letting a ground ball go through his legs to lose Game Six in extra innings. The Mets claimed the championship by winning Game Seven).

Hence, I was shifting between the kitchen and the living room throughout the evening.

I started making the pumpkin pie filling but was stumped when the recipe called for egg whites. Egg whites? I didn't know how to get egg whites on their own. I had only used entire eggs for recipes.

I had only ever seen egg whites one way: hard-boiled.

I try to blame my mother for my lack of knowledge, since

she had taught my three sisters how to cook but didn't have time to teach me.

No one buys that excuse, either.

So, I immersed two eggs in a pot of water, heated up the stove, and headed back to immerse myself in the World Series.

Forty-five minutes later, I heard a whistling noise coming from the kitchen, much like a tea kettle. I wasn't boiling tea, so what could the sound be . . . oh, right, I was boiling eggs, wasn't I?

Returning to the kitchen, I found all the water had boiled away, and the eggs had holes burned through their shells, so the whistling was the sound of air escaping.

I yanked the pan off the stove and immediately started peeling the eggs. As you can imagine, they were quite hot.

I reached for a knife to chop up the egg whites to put them in the pumpkin mixture. The first egg white was very hot and gummy, so chopping was difficult. For the second egg, I simply peeled off the egg white and mushed it up in my fingers – Hot! Hot! – then dropped it into the mixture.

After beating the pumpkin mixture, it still appeared . . . lumpy, let's say. My solution? I should dump the mixture in the blender! Now, I had no idea what speed to blend it, so I used all the speeds. I drove that blender like an eighteen-wheeler, shifting through the gears – rrrr, rrrr – with different sounds and activities happening inside the swirl. Finally, I figured the mixture had suffered enough, and I poured it into the pie shell.

This is a good time to mention that we had a cantankerous oven. Often it would just start overheating; if you set it at three hundred-fifty degrees, it might run up as high as five hundred degrees. If the oven was having a bad day, baking was a sequence of turning the oven off and on to try to maintain the desired temperature. You had to keep an eye on it.

I didn't keep an eye on it. I was keeping an eye on a tense, exciting World Series Game Six.

I popped the pie in the oven, intending to return in fifty minutes to retrieve it.

Seventy minutes later, my nose reminded me that I had a pie in the oven. I raced out of the living room, trading the drama of the World Series for certain drama in the kitchen, as I expected a charred pie.

Surprisingly, it wasn't charred, despite a small amount of overheating and baking way too long. However, perhaps due to the excessive air introduced by the blender, the pie had puffed up several inches. Actually, it reminded me of a Mayan temple. It had steps and slopes and perhaps even a little dugout at the top. Maybe I was just seeing baseball visions everywhere.

I pulled out the pie and gently poked it. Poooooof! The air came out of the pie, and the surface descended. The temple was no more.

Now came an interesting part. This was a sugar-free pie, and I was using an artificial sweetener. In those days, artificial sweeteners couldn't be baked; they became carcinogenic in the process, which didn't seem like a good result for a birthday pie. So the sweetener had to be added after the baking. I lined up eight packets of sweetener to add to the pie.

Let me pause and ask a question that has been an ongoing debate between Sara and me, even decades later. In fact, we frequently ask this question of friends. How would you add the sweetener packets to the pie?

Most people say they would sprinkle the eight packets over the pie and mix it all up together. But I was too rigidly mathematical for that.

Instead, I took one packet, calculated one-eighth of the pie, and stirred the packet into that area. I repeated the process for all eight sections of the pie. (To Sara, this is as funny as any part of the story.)

Naturally, the pie surface was rugged — rugged like a lava field and still nearly as hot. I smoothed it out, much like swirling the icing onto a cake. It wasn't the best-looking pie, but it looked like a pumpkin pie. Sort of.

The job was done in time to watch the stunning finish to Game Six.

The next morning, Sara called up her best friend, Teri, to tell her what I had done. Teri was married to a hefty chef named Miltos.

Here's the scenario: I was standing in our kitchen. Sara was on the phone in our living room. Teri was in her living room. Miltos was cooking in their kitchen while Teri related the details to him. I could hear Miltos laughing loudly . . . all the way from his kitchen, through the rooms and the phones, and into my kitchen!

Finally, I'd had enough of this ridicule. I told Sara she should eat the pumpkin pie right now, with Teri on the phone. Sara was hesitant. But I cut a slice and served it to her.

Sara took a bite and began laughing again.

I asked, "Is it that bad?"

Still chewing, she said, "No! It's the best pumpkin pie I've ever had!"

Christmas 1986 brought me four gag gifts from various members of our families: egg separators.

I never made the pie again without properly separating the eggs. After all, Bill Buckner and I have to own our mistakes and move forward.

~ 30 ~

Using My Karate Chops in Nursing

Susan Schwartz

I was called to the main desk in the OR department at the beginning of my shift because there was a problem with a patient. A couple of the staff knew I took Tang Soo Do, a Korean martial art, and thought I might be of valuable assistance.

Now, I know what you are thinking: We had a belligerent patient who needed to be subdued in order to save another staff member. Or, maybe it was a hostage situation, and I needed to go in like Chuck Norris and save the day with my famous roundhouse kick.

Well . . . it was actually something I had never imagined.

She was a sweet, eighty-seven-year-old Korean lady, looking lost and confused because she spoke no English. Her daughter was with her in the pre-op area trying to help until a translator could arrive. Since I knew enough Korean from my martial arts to be dangerous, I tried to assist in keeping them as comfortable as possible before her outpatient procedure.

Stepping into the woman's room, I ˙said, "Annyeong-hashimnikka" (formal hello in Korean). She grinned and waved at me. She quickly started to talk and I explained to her daughter that although I was not fluent in Korean, I did know a few words and phrases. I wanted to try to help her mother through the procedure so she didn't feel all alone in a strange place. The daughter was very grateful that I would take the time to do such a time-consuming task for her mother. I told her that no patient should ever feel alone, especially in an operating room. When it was time to head for her surgery, I walked back to the OR with her, repeating "shio" (relax, be calm).

When we arrived in the OR, we got the beds lined up perfectly and the wheels locked in place. The CRNA looked at me and said, "Do your magic."

I patted the OR table and told the lady, "Ahn Jo," (sit here).

She slid over to the table as I directed her to move her "pahl," then her "bahl," (move her arms at the top, then her feet at the bottom to scoot over to the OR table). When she was on the table and situated, I again said, "Shio." She smiled and nodded.

I stayed with her and held her hand, reminding her to "shio" throughout the procedure of being prepared for sleep. She chatted with me the whole time, and although I had no idea what she was saying, I could tell she was happy to have someone that could speak to her and give her simple directions she could understand. She went off to sleep quite easily.

After the procedure, I returned, to be there when she awoke. She remembered me and smiled. I again said, "Annyeong-hashimnikka. Shio." The CRNA took time to get her completely awake so she would be ready for her daughter and the translator to come to recovery and stay with her. Until then, I stayed and held her hand. She was sleepy from the anesthesia, but seemed at peace, knowing we were going to take good care of her and keep her safe.

After she arrived in recovery, her daughter came to sit with her, and I explained what had happened in the interim. Her mother had been through a frightening situation with someone who spoke only a little of her language. I went back to check her about an hour later, and she was getting ready to return home. She stood, and with a bow said, "Ko Map Sum Ni Da," (thank you very much).

I returned her bow with "Chomane yo," (you're welcome).

I learned that even the smallest thing we do for a patient will sometimes be of the greatest help. This patient was able to go through an important and frightening procedure knowing she was not lost and alone, but with a nurse who could communicate with her, using a few words learned in a karate class.

It made all the difference in the world.

~ 31 ~

Lost and Frazzled

Christina Sinisi

Somehow, when brainstorming for a story I'd like to share in this book, I recalled one that is both literal and underlying with deeper meaning.

In other words, I was truly, about-to-lose-my-mind lost.

I could not find my way and I had a vanload of young people depending on me.

As a professor of Psychology at Charleston Southern University, a small Baptist-affiliated university, for over two decades I coaxed, encouraged, and drove students to conferences where they could network with other students and faculty as well as present their research. I still teach there, but I've shared that wonderful experience of chaperoning students at conferences with younger faculty members now.

Taking turns is a skill I learned a long time ago.

One of the conferences we attended for many years was the Carolinas Undergraduate Conference, held in Raleigh, North Carolina at the time. I can't remember what my husband had going on that particular year, but I took both of my children with me. My son was about five and my daughter was a toddler still in a car seat. My sister met me the next day and babysat.

The students carpooled up I-95 and we met at the hotel. Rather than driving separate cars around a strange city, we all piled into my minivan. It was a green Toyota, with a sliding side door, three seats in the back, Lindsey's car seat in the middle with one student beside her and two of us up front.

This was before the days of GPS and cell phones.

We had a map, but it was the one provided by the conference, drawn by people who knew their way around. We found the restaurant just fine — Cheesecake Factory for the win. So, at least we had food in our bellies and wouldn't die of starvation if we never found our way back.

In April, the interstate in Raleigh is covered with azalea blooms and apple blossoms, but dusk was looming, making signs harder to see. The conference switched yearly between North Carolina State and Meredith College. The former is a behemoth, state university and the latter is a small, women's college. We were able to find North Carolina State but not the psychology building, where we were to register.

We listened to Veggie Tales while driving around in circles. College students singing "Where's My Hairbrush?" with your children to keep them entertained is a gift you never forget.

My contacts had my eyes itchy and scratchy. I had trouble with my peripheral vision. We kept going around in circles for quite a while, missing a side exit until someone finally saw it. The frustration wore at us despite the quality musical interludes, punctuated with tense silence.

Finally, I found a spot in a parking lot and we all got out. We walked around, looking for directions. When we found a sign . . . it told us we were on the wrong side of campus.

It was dark and everyone was exhausted. But, at least knowing we were on the wrong side of campus meant we knew where we were and where we needed to go. Checking our watches, we saw we had just enough time to pile back into our seats and make it to the registration desk.

The problem was, a large bus, a literal team bus, was now blocking the only exit to the parking lot.

Lindsey, or maybe one of the college students, started to cry. I was having enough difficulty breathing that tears were out of the question for me.

Heather, the student sitting next to Lindsey, held my daughter's hand, and asked if she could pray.

Pray? Of course!

She prayed and we all calmed down a bit. The bus moved. We drove, and the students got registered in time.

Sometimes, when we're well and truly lost — we wandered for hours, not forty years, but it was still painful — help comes from unexpected places. For instance, I'd never have expected a college student to step up and ask to pray when I certainly was too frazzled to go to the source. But help can always come from a very expected place — our Lord and Savior.

We asked and He led.

I now have multiple hairbrushes (thanks, Bob, the tomato), a cell phone, and GPS. But most importantly, I also know to go to the source when I need help.

Oh, and about Heather: She went on to become a Christian speaker and published writer who inspires people with her faith.

Leadership shows up in many ways.

Amen!

~ 32 ~

Searching for the Lost

Vicki H. Moss

My dear Mother used to hide some of her possessions from her children to keep us from using them. Scissors for instance. She didn't want children dulling the blades with paper because dull blades chewed fabric when used to make garments. The problem was, after hiding the scissors, she couldn't recall where she'd put them and they stayed lost for months.

Searching for Mother's scissors made me vow I'd never lose things when I grew up.

It's laughable now. Because after I had children of my own I couldn't recall where I'd put anything or even if I might have possibly lost something. I was especially negligent when it came to jewelry. I lost a bracelet while shopping in Oxford, Mississippi once and retraced my steps in the town square several times, inquiring in every store about my lost treasure. No luck. After searching dressing rooms I'd been in, cracks in concrete sidewalks, and patches of well-manicured grass, I finally gave up and darkened the door of The City Grocery restaurant to put some salve on my wound by forking shrimp and grits onto my taste buds. Not even shrimp and grits could ease the pain of the loss of that bracelet, however.

Then there's the ongoing issue I have with the verse that tells me that as a follower of Christ, I "have the mind of Christ." If I have the mind of Christ (Who is omniscient and omnipresent), then Jesus, please show me where I lost that bracelet.

Nothing.

Recently, I misplaced a special ring. A favorite ring I'd worn for years. I remember telling myself I needed to put it in a better hiding place because I know thieves do break in; but like Mother with her scissors, I couldn't recall where the better place was. I searched high. Then low. Then all around. In cubbies. In corners. I searched everywhere for that elusive ring and could not find it.

Then I heard as plain as day in my spirit, "Would you search as hard for me as you are searching for that ring?" Aghast, I replied, "You know I would Lord! Where did that even come from? You know I love you and have been seeking you ever since I was six years old. Studying your Word. Praying. Bullet prayers while in the car driving. How could you even ask that? Have I not been a servant? Well, most of the time? *Some* of the time?"

But a thought instantly popped into my head and the thought pained me more than the lost ring. *Well, if I'm ultra honest, I have gotten slack with my prayers lately. It's so easy to simply say, "Lord, bless the entire world, bring everyone to Christ so all can go to heaven. You know what everyone needs, especially heal the sick, and take care of the little ones. Bless us all indeed, ditto the prayer I said yesterday, and Amen."*

And before I forget, there's that pain I get when I kneel — do I have to bend the knee every time when I pray before bed? Yes, I know it helps me focus better when I'm on my knees but you know how my face starts itching and all I want to do is scratch.

No answer.

I then I thought about *how* I was praying. I wasn't thanking and praising enough. There were times when I was so hungry I wolfed down my food before even remembering I had forgotten to pray a prayer of thanksgiving, then felt guilty for not remembering to pray because I was thinking about my stomach more than I was thinking about my job down here on earth — to help win souls for Christ.

Am I not praying long enough? Eloquently enough? Not using the correct phraseology because I'm not using your favorite Bible translation? What is my exact job down here on my patch of ground anyway? This place is so hard to figure out. Don't pass go. Do pass go. *Okay, Lord, I'll try to do better. And I have been searching for you diligently — but it's really difficult when I can't look at you — have you seated in front of me over breakfast coffee or elderberry tea. You get that not being visible causes so many to backslide. I'm only human. I can't be the only filthy rag down here who is derelict in earthly duties. And yes, I'm aware there are a ton of lost people around me. But I'm just one person. What more would you have me do? Can you send me an email and lay it all out for me? Bullet points on a month-by-month calendar would help tremendously.*

And then, I feel like He's just — gone. If He was ever there. And I'm left alone again to figure everything out by myself it seems.

And how quickly my mind starts to wander. To writing, for heaven's sake. I think I've written every Christmas story I can ever write. What else could I ever write about Christmas? Why did that even pop into my ever-lovin mind?

Then I heard in my spirit: Christmas Tree Skirt. *Aha! Lord, you're still here. And yes, I've never written about the Christmas tree skirt I made years ago. Just when I thought you were no longer with me, you give me another great idea. When will I learn that your Word is a living Word?*

Once again, Nothing. But that one idea is enough. And that's the way I'm supposed to live. One step at a time it seems. For now.

Who knows, maybe, eventually, while I'm searching for the lost I'll be told where that favorite lost ring is.

And when she has found it, she calls together her friends and neighbors, saying, "Rejoice with me, for I have found the coin that I had lost." Just so, I tell you, there is joy before the angels of God over one sinner who repents. Luke 15:9-10 ESV

33

Zoe

Beverly Hill McKinney

Hey, Bev," called my big sister, Zoe, "if you want to go see Mrs. Charles' fish pond and pretty flowers, we should go now."

I jumped up and ran outside as fast as my four-year-old legs would carry me. My sister, twenty-two months older than me, was always ready for an adventure together.

"Mrs. Charles got some pretty new fish to put in her pond," I said to my mom and rushed past my sister out the door.

"Wait!" Mom called. "You know I want Zoe to hold your hand after last time when you ran out in the street."

"Okay, but hurry, I really want to see the fish, and she even has some new flowers."

Zoe was the third child in the family; I was the youngest. My parents were older when I was born and both had busy lives. Since my two brothers were several years older, my sister became my nearest and dearest friend. We shared a special bond that I always feel is reserved for sisters.

My protector! From the time I was quite small I always thought of my sister as my protector. Whenever crossing the street Zoe was always there to hold my hand. Since we lived in a small town, we often walked hand in hand downtown to the large Five and Dime store to just look at all the treasures.

"Come on Bev, let's go to the beach," Zoe called one hot sunny day.

"Oh boy! We can watch crabs under the rocks and take Blackie (our dog) with us."

"As long as you promise me not to wander off or let Blackie drink the sea water, because it will him sick."

"I promise," I said.

It seemed through life Zoe was always there to "hold my hand." The Lord gave us a closeness that we shared whether in person or through long telephone conversations, lengthy letters when we lived states apart, or small words of encouragement that came during dark hours in my life. Sometimes we called each other just because we had a "feeling" we needed to talk.

We were also best buddies and friends.

My father built Zoe and I a playhouse in our backyard using a large moving crate. He set it on a cement foundation and even added a shingled roof. Zoe and I shared many hours of fun and happiness in that playhouse. We were scientists who collected bugs, oceanographers who collected "specimens" from Monterey Bay near our home, evangelists who held church services for all the neighbor kids.

One of the saddest days of my life came soon after my parents had passed away. One day as were in the process of selling their home, I drove by it. To my horror, our wonderful playhouse had been removed. I grieved because it meant now I really had only the memories.

Zoe also kept me from harm during our adventures. Near our home was a large pine forest where water settled into small swamps after the rains. The area was known as Nine Ponds because of all of its little pools. It was a dangerous area, filled with lots of rotten logs, crumbing dirt, and mud. When I was very young, Zoe always held my hand while we were there, and as we grew older she stayed by my side while we were busy exploring. I well remember the two of us trudging through Nine Ponds in search of pollywogs to take home to raise. I can't count the number of frogs we grew from those small pollywogs and then released in my parents' large vegetable garden.

Zoe also helped me spiritually. She always had a deep faith. When I became impulsive and wanted to run ahead of the Lord, she patiently helped me and prayed for me to find my way back. Because of this, I consistently knew that throughout my life if I had a spiritual need I could count on her.

Because of our closeness in age, Zoe and I attended the same church youth camp. One summer, barely into the first week, I became quite ill. But I wanted to stay at camp.

"Bev," Zoe said, "you know you're too sick to stay. I'm calling the folks. I'm really worried about you."

"Oh no, please don't call," I begged. "I really love camp. I don't want to go home."

"I know, but you're too sick," she insisted.

She immediately phoned my parents and asked them to come the one hundred miles to pick me up because she was so worried about me. She even wanted to go home with me but my parents insisted she stay and enjoy the camp. Although I hated to admit she was right, my parents were a welcome sight.

We lived in a small community with one grammar school and high school. Zoe was two grades ahead of me in school.

When she graduated from grammar school and went to high school I was lonely and had a difficult time. Then, as my first day of high school approached, I was very nervous. I hesitantly walked up to the front door with a girlfriend, and there was Zoe waiting for us! She was there as a big junior to help her little freshman sister feel more at home. Two years later she left for college, and even though inheriting her bedroom was a bright spot in the adventure, for a brief time my world seemed to stop.

As Zoe and I grew older and married, we lived far apart for a while. Yet she was always there to send me words of encouragement or call just to talk. Since we were both serving the Lord in various ministries, we often phoned each other with ideas and suggestions. What a precious time of sharing that was!

Zoe has gone to be with the Lord now. When she passed away, I wrote the following poem in her memory.

My Sister, My Protector, My Buddy, My Friend

When we were young you were always there
holding my hand — I was in your care.
Venturing out you would watch with concern,
ready to snatch me to ground that was firm.
You were my protector, my buddy, my friend.

As we got older, we still had great fun
catching pollywogs or frogs up at Nine Ponds.
Playing in the playhouse was, for me, constant joy!
Or Sunday rides catching horned toads and more.
You were my protector, my buddy, my friend.

When you went to High School I did miss you so.
All alone I was left at the Grammar School.
I felt the loss of my big sis even more, but
You still were my protector, my buddy, my friend.

At High School we were together once again.
You being there to help me blend in.
I felt secure knowing you were there.
You were my protector, my buddy, my friend

When you went to college and left me at home,
I missed you, my sister, my buddy, my friend.
You were living so far, far away, to me,
even though I got your room for free!
You were my protector, my buddy, my friend.

As I married and we lived many miles apart,
I always knew I was held in your heart.
I could always call you and share my concerns;
you were there to give kudos when they were earned.
You were my protector, my buddy, my friend.

Now that you have left for your journey on high,
Getting to see our Lord, with your very eyes,
I'll always remember the times that we shared,
You holding my hand, and all of your care,
I miss you so much,
My Sister, My Protector, My Buddy, My Friend.

34

Lost in Reception

Lola Di Giulio De Maci

My husband came home from work one day with one of life's many dilemmas. His supervisor wanted him to transfer to another department, but he wanted to stay right where he was.

"I need to give him an answer in the morning. I don't know what to do," he told me.

"Sometimes in life you just have to make a decision," I said. "Search your heart. Sleep on it. And then you just have to pick and choose."

"Chicken snooze?" he replied, his brow furrowed.

"Chicken snooze?" I questioned. "What's a chicken snooze?"

He stood before me bewildered. "Isn't that what you said?"

Truth be told, my husband didn't always hear exactly what I said. He heard exactly what he heard (or wanted to hear).

The previous day I had asked him to order me a classic chicken burrito when he went through our neighborhood's drive-thru. He called me several minutes later. "They don't have a plastic chicken," he stated matter-of-factly.

"Plastic chicken!" I said, trying to hold back my frustration. "I said a *classic* chicken burrito, not a *plastic* one.

"Oh," he replied.

And so it went, time after time.

It all started one day at lunch when I asked him if he wanted a bunch of grapes with his grilled cheese sandwich.

"Leslie Ape?" he questioned. "Who's Leslie Ape?"

"Leslie Ape?!" *I* questioned. "Who said anything about a Leslie Ape? I said 'a bunch of grapes.' "

When it came time to launder the rugs, I gathered all the throw rugs throughout the house and put them in the washer. Instead of taxing my dryer, I hung them outside over the patio furniture. The summer sun was hot enough to do its part.

"I think the rugs are dry now," I called my dutiful husband. "Would you mind bringing them in?"

He appeared almost instantly in the family room with a fly swatter in hand.

"What bugs are flying in?" he asked.

I wished he could have somehow used that flyswatter. The whole situation would have made a lot more sense.

At the end of one exhausting day, we headed to our favorite sandwich shop. We selected the table closest to a window — our preferred spot in the coziest part of the room. Looking over the menu, I offered my beloved husband a meaty suggestion: "Want to share a chicken sandwich?"

"What about Stonewall Jackson?" he asked.

"Stonewall Jackson! Who said anything about Stonewall Jackson?" I laid my head in my hands, praying that I hadn't really heard what he'd just said.

That day, bite by bite, we bid a fond adieu to The General who'd joined us for lunch.

It would have been a lot less entertaining if he hadn't shown up.

~ 35 ~

Lost and Found

Helen L. Hoover

"Mother, I can't find my ruby ring," Ginger tearfully told me one morning. "I've looked everywhere."

"When did you last have it?" I asked.

"I don't know for sure. It's been missing for a couple of weeks. I thought I'd find it. I didn't want to have to tell you and Dad. I've searched my room and car from top to bottom."

"Well, honey, let's pray that God will guide you to it. He knows where it is and loves you very much."

The ring was Ginger's prized possession. Larry and I had given it to her for her high school graduation gift. She wore it almost constantly, so it was a mystery as to how she could have misplaced it.

For several days, her two younger brothers, her Dad, and I were vigilant to look around the house and our vehicles for the ring. But to no avail.

A couple of months later, our family went to see my dad and his wife. We hadn't visited since Christmas, so we needed to check on them. My stepmother is a good housekeeper, but she has one lamp table with a shelf at the bottom that holds magazines and newspapers stacked at various angles and heights as people read and then put them back. The unruly periodicals are left on the shelf for several months for visitors to have a chance to read them or take them home.

On this visit, my parents had been sharing their plans for the coming summer and we were telling them about our activities since we had visited with them at Christmastime.

Ginger sat in a chair by the lamp table. "Oh, look!" we heard her exclaim suddenly, "Here's my ring!"

"Where'd you find it?" her dad asked.

"I looked down to get a magazine and it was just lying here on the edge of the magazine. How could that happen?"

We were all as surprised as she was.

"Do you suppose it's been lying there since Christmas?" I wondeed aloud.

"I don't know. I wouldn't have taken it off my finger and put it there," was her reply.

"I doubt that it has been there since Christmas," my stepmother said. "We often look at those magazines and then put them back on the shelf."

"Wow! God came through for you honey," I told her. "He answered our prayer. You are special to Him and He knew the ring was special to you."

We were all in awe and wonder at how God showed Ginger her ring. It seems doubtful that the ring had been lying on the magazine since Christmas. It remains a mystery. But it is no mystery that God loves His children and does special things for them, even finding a lost item.

Hebrews 1:14 tells us angels are sent to serve Christians. Had an angel put the ring on the magazine so Ginger would see it? Had it lain there for over two months? How had it not fallen off when other items were removed and replaced? Why hadn't someone seen it before our visit? It's interesting that she chose to sit in the chair on that side of the table during our visit.

We will probably never know the answers to our questions. What we do know is that God cares for His children.

36

Salvaging What's Lost

Laura Sweeney

JUNE 2018

I made an inventory of what was missing from the storage unit. The list was long. Almost everything of value that someone could possibly pawn or sell on eBay was gone.

The mantel clock Stepfather carved for each of us. A striped and polka dotted hippo collection hand-painted by my nephew, inspired by the song "I Want a Hippopotamus for Christmas." A cross, blessed by a Guatemalan priest in la Basílica de Esquipulas, home of the Black Christ. The cross necklace my father had hand-carved for me. The cheese grater Mom brought from Norway. A ceramic platter and two coffee cups bought in Colima when my sister had E. coli. The ballerina music box Grandma J. gave me as a teen. A Russian music box no bigger than a quarter that played "Lara's Theme" from *Dr. Zhivago*. A bright pink Indian box, bought at Worldly Goods with my volunteer's discount. A puzzle box shaped like the quetzal, Guatemala's national bird, bought on a research trip. A mosaic pillbox. Two Russian lacquer boxes. The hairpin and barrette collection — one Russian, carved from wood, another Nicaraguan turtle shell. *What might those have been worth?* The silver watch with the Sandburg quote "time is the coin of your life" Mom had given me. The gold Swiss watch a boyfriend bought me during a conference on The Continent, still in its red box. A necklace from India, made from a rupee. An African ivory necklace passed down from Grandma S. — I had never found an occasion to wear yet.

On the storage unit floor I found the ribbon that had wrapped the velvet-lined silver box that encased Grandma Great's pearls. The pearls she had worn on her wedding day. The pearls I had inherited on my sixteenth birthday to wear on my own wedding day, and had fought to keep when I left home at eighteen. *I should have placed them in a safety deposit box.*

But other things were also missing. Sentimental, decorative pieces: a blown-glass vase from Aunt Jo; the hand-carved Eskimo sled and huskie from adventures Grandpa S. had while helping build the Alaskan railroad; the tea set with an apple design sent from a roommate who'd moved to New York; a Mardi Gras doll I'd bought in the New Orleans French Quarter.

For years I had displayed these items on a shelf I intended to refurbish the way I had my cherry wood table that still sat in the storage shed corner. My efforts on that had won a ribbon at the State Fair. Next to it lay a piece of lock and a piece of cork from the Biltmore Riesling I'd saved for graduation.

Dumbfounded, I described the burglary to my Southern Illinois University counselor. Douglas had become my therapist during my first semester at SIU when my blood pressure had skyrocketed as the Chancellor, believing enrollment was low because undergrads didn't want to study with graduate instructors, enlisted volunteers from the college and community to teach courses, serve on committees, and review theses "for the experience" rather than paying faculty to do it. With two masters degrees, I qualified as an instructor of record, akin to an adjunct; but as a woman in my cohort had observed, we were being weeded out. She had gone back to Germany, to a future in horse grooming. Others had left, too. Now, after a year, Douglas was one of the few allies I had left on campus.

He reminded me of a sermon by Father Cedric, an SIU alum. "Bad luck or good luck, crud or the cup?" he challenged. "It's all in how you frame it."

He guided me through a breathing exercise, similar to the one I had been taught at the Women of Wisdom retreat in Rock Island, Illinois, where I had spent an early June weekend on my way north to Ames and my storage unit.

Inhale good stuff, exhale bad stuff.

I thought of the storage units' manager to whom I had reported the robbery. Stunned by the mess of overturned boxes that greeted me upon removing the broken padlock, I had stormed to the front office. The manager had been nonchalant. "Everybody thinks it won't happen to them but when it does, it's like losing grandmother's pearls."

There'd been a rash of robberies, he explained. They'd found a suspect on camera but hadn't caught him. He advised me to call the sheriff and file a report. The sheriff offered to call the area pawnshops, but nothing came of it.

Of course, I questioned myself about choosing that particular storage place on the outskirts of Ames. It was independently owned and operated, with no security fence. I hadn't done my homework. In an attempt to leave behind traumatic events I had loaded the unit, packed my car to the gills, and fled with my dog,

Freya, to southern Illinois.

As I shared my fiasco with Douglas and lamented the loss, he offered empathy. "I don't own much either. I packed everything and moved south, too." He had moved cross-country from Oregon to Massachusetts for his PhD, to Texas for his post-doc, and now southern Illinois for his assistant professorship.

"You knew this was going to be hard," he said, as I continued to express my frustrations. "But I'll sit in the muck of it all with you. Is this rock bottom?

"Self-care," he said. "The work you do on yourself is the work you do on the world." The magazines in the student health center were full of articles about self-care, the new buzzword.

I was reminded about the poem "Kindness" by one of my favorite writers, Naomi Shihab Nye, which appeared in her first full-length collection. While on her honeymoon in South America, she and her husband were robbed. No money, no friends, no passport. The only thing she had left was a notebook and pencil. So she sat in a public plaza and wrote.

"You have something to contribute. You're a writer," Douglas had told me. "They'd have to drag me out kicking and screaming. Don't leave without what you came here for. Writing and exercise are your weapons."

True, I always believed you can lose everything in life, but nobody can take away your education or your publications. Samizdat, as they say. Get your work out there any which way you can.

I took Douglas' mantra about self-care to heart.

After all, I had my Freya and our walks in the Shawnee National Forest. Time to meditate on how far we had come, and the fact that God hadn't brought us this far to leave us now. With nothing but faith as an anchor to cling to, we had launched into the deep for a reason.

As I walked, I repeated two things: The reason I'm here is not the reason I'm here. And my favorite Bible verse, Jeremiah 6:16: I stand at the crossroads, consider the ancient paths, ask what is the good way, and walk in it to find rest for my soul. (Author's paraphrase)

MAY 2020

I defended my MFA via a Zoom conference in the midst of the COVID shutdown, graduating into the Great Pandemic. The focus of my presentation: Psychological sturdiness. So much of the world was suffering such great loss. It was all out of our hands. Yes, it was evil.

Like the line in the movie *Wall Street*, I was that woman who looked into the abyss with nothing staring back. But in the process, I found grit. And that is what got me through my MFA program and the pandemic.

But I was also like the woman in Kings who thought she had nothing to share or contribute to the world yet was advised to ask her neighbors for empty jars, pour her olive oil into the containers, then distribute abundantly.

Throughout my MFA program, rather than feel sorry for myself and my losses I spent hours writing and revising followed by more hours submitting to small-press journals.

OCTOBER 2023

Now, three years later, I reflect on these things as I sit at my French bistro table, a wrought iron patio set I bought in the East

Village in Des Moines. The price tag still hangs from the chair. I consider the Nefertiti portrait from my grandmother's funeral, and the cat-with-nine-lives lithograph I bought in the market in Cuba. Soon I will decorate with Christmas decorations and a portrait of Santa's Castle from Storm Lake, Iowa, my hometown.

All are items salvaged from my storage shed.

As I reflect upon my losses and subsequent progress I realize no one can take away my spirit of determination, my will to carry on if I trust God and keep moving forward with Him.

37

Only Five Minutes

Sheryl Boldt

I was sitting in the clinic waiting room leafing through a magazine when a piercing sound erupted from the intercom.

"CODE BLUE! CODE BLUE! CODE BLUE!"

Like a scene from a hospital drama, the loudspeaker blasted its urgent message throughout the clinic. A doctor, his white coat flapping, raced around the corner, almost colliding with two nurses pushing a crash cart. Flinging the treatment room door open, they shoved the cart through the doorway and disappeared.

I sat in stunned silence, frightened for the kind-eyed older man who'd walked through those doors just minutes earlier.

I'd been waiting for a friend when I felt a sense of urgency to speak to the man, who was sitting nearby.

"Hello," I began.

Mr. Jenkins returned my greeting, and we entered easily into a conversation. We talked about superficial things — grandchildren and the weather — yet I became increasingly uncomfortable. In my spirit, I felt the Holy Spirit urging me to ask him a question.

"Mr. Jenkins," I said, taking a deep breath, "would you mind if I ask you a personal question?"

Thankfully, my voice sounded more confident than I felt.

"No . . . I don't mind."

"If today were the last day of your life, where will you spend eternity?"

He smiled when he said, "Because of Jesus' death on the cross for my sins, I'll spend eternity in heaven." He lowered his gaze and sighed. His graying mustache twitched as he continued, "I'm worried about my son, Scott. He's very reluctant to pursue a closer relationship with God. Recently when I talked to him about it, he changed the subject and asked me if we could talk about something else."

He spoke more about Scott — his recent marriage, his love for sports, and his passion for cars. "He just opened his own mechanic shop," Mr. Jenkins said with a proud smile.

"Would it be okay if I prayed for Scott?" I asked. He nodded.

"Father, please make yourself real to Scott," I prayed. "Help him know how much he needs you. We pray that he will commit his heart and life to you soon."

Mr. Jenkins' quiet, "Amen," echoed my own.

"Mr. Jenkins?" a technician called, entering the waiting area. He smiled warmly at me before stepping through the radiology room door. Two minutes later the alarm sounded, and five minutes later, Mr. Jenkins was dead.

Numb with shock and overwhelmed with emotions, I sat there, unable to move. The very man I'd asked, only minutes before, where he would spend eternity was now standing before God in heaven. *Is this why I felt compelled to speak to Mr. Jenkins? Was it God's plan for him to have one final opportunity to pray for his son?*

That night, I shared my experience with my Bible study group. "It scares me to think how easily I could have ignored God," I said. "I can't help but wonder how many times I've missed His divine appointments."

"I know," my friend Kathy said. "Sometimes I get so caught up with my own agenda that, frankly, I feel too busy to take time to stop and listen to God."

"Let's pray and ask God to make us more sensitive to His voice," said another friend.

After we prayed, I sensed a new urging. I knew I had to find Scott and tell him about my conversation with his father.

Recalling bits of information I'd received from Mr. Jenkins, I located Scott's mechanic shop. I waited a couple of weeks to allow Scott to mourn, then drove into the small gravel parking lot alongside a worn, metal-framed building. A man was busy working under the hood of a late-model Ford.

Watching him, my heart pounded. *God, I'm really nervous.* I put my hand on the stick shift, intending to put the car into reverse, but continued to pray. *Lord, I need you. Please give me courage.* I removed my hand from the gearshift and opened the door.

"Hello," I said to the man, "I'm looking for Scott Jenkins."

"That's me," he said. "How can I help you?"

"Hi, Scott, my name is Sheryl." A pause . . . *What do I say now?* "I can see you're busy, but I wanted to meet you." Taking a deep breath, I continued, "I met your father recently, and he told me so much about you. Do you have a few minutes?"

He nodded, closed the hood of the car, and wiped his hands with the rag hanging from his greased-stained overalls. Folding his muscular arms across his chest, he waited for me to speak.

Another deep breath, "Scott, I was in the same waiting room with your father at the medical center just before he died. He talked a lot about you. He mentioned how proud he was of you owning your own mechanic shop."

"Hmmm?" His eyebrows lifted, pleased and curious.

"He also mentioned something that troubled him. Your father was concerned about your relationship with God. In fact, just before he went in to get his X-ray, he prayed that you would understand how much you needed God, and that God would make himself real to you."

"Hmmm." This time he sounded lost in thought.

I paused, giving him time to think. "Do you have any questions?"

He gave a slight nod, staring blankly at the oil-smeared floor. "Did he look sick?"

"No. He looked fine to me. Actually, he looked like a proud father who really loved his son. I could tell, because he smiled a lot when he talked about you." After a few seconds, I continued. "Scott, would you spend some time thinking about your dad's last prayer for you?"

He looked at me with a sad smile and nodded. "Yeah. Sure." He stuck out his hand, and I did, too. "Thank you for coming."

Reaching my car, I took a deep breath and exhaled slowly. *Father, please be with Scott during this time. Help him appreciate his father's prayers. I pray, Lord, that Scott will come to know you and love you like his father did.*

I moved to Florida a few months later, and I lost track of Scott. I often wonder what became of him, but I'm learning to trust God's sovereignty. Although I didn't get to see how this story ends, I'm thankful I followed through with what God called me to do. And I know God will use others to further the work He allowed me to be a part of.

The next time you sense the prompting of the Holy Spirit, I hope you'll think of Mr. Jenkins. Who would have thought only five minutes would stand between our prayer and his eternity?

~ 38 ~

Charlie Greene's Long Race to Faith

Robert B. Robeson

To many followers of the international track scene in the 1960s and early 1970s, Charles Edward ("Charlie") Greene was arrogant, egotistical and flippant. He was a world-class African-American sprinter who wore flashy clothes and was quick with a quip. His trademarks on the track were ever-present sunglasses and the "thumbs-up" gesture he often employed when crossing the finish line. But the most important factor, then, for this five-foot seven-inch lightning bolt was the fact he could mash everyone else in the world for sixty to one hundred meters.

Charlie began to make a name for himself after whipping-off a 9.8-second hundred-yard dash as a one hundred-twenty-five-pound high school sophomore in Seattle, Washington. As a senior, he ignited the track at the 1963 Golden West Invitational Track Meet in California with a 9.4 clocking in the hundred-yard final. That earned him the number one high school sprinter rating in the nation.

He then accepted a four-year track scholarship to the University of Nebraska in Lincoln. In his freshman year, the world record in the sixty-yard dash was six seconds flat. After training for just three weeks, he ran it in 6.1.

In February of 1964, Charlie ran in the AAU (Amateur Athletic Union) Track Meet in New York City. Before the final of the sixty-yard dash he informed "Bullet" Bob Hayes, another of the greatest sprinters in history whom he'd never met, "Bobby, if you beat me, you'll have to set a world record to do it."

That's exactly what Hayes did. He finished with a 5.9-second clocking and Charlie tied the previous world record of 6.0.

Charlie's incessant chatter before races compelled some to refer to him as "Chirpin' Charlie." During the finals of college sprints he developed a tactic to "get into the other sprinters' heads." Charlie would make an announcement, "Gentlemen, my name's Charlie Greene and I've already got first place. The rest of you guys need to figure out who's going to get second." He admitted he was supremely confident. He went three straight years, from 1965 to 1968, without losing a sixty- or hundred-yard dash.

His sunglasses, crazy quotes and other antics garnered him more media recognition than most other athletes. He admitted to being a "status seeker." It was always his intention to use his tart tongue to get attention.

This hotshot flash held four world sprint records at the same time in the 1960s. Then, as a member of the 1968 (Mexico City) U.S. Olympic team, Charlie added a gold medal (440-meter relay) and a bronze medal to his already impressive credentials.

Charlie pulled a hamstring muscle halfway through the 100-meter final and had to settle for third place. Still injured, he ran the 440-meter relay preliminaries a few days later. He froze the muscle with ice minutes before the final. The U.S. team set a world record of 38.19 seconds. This record stood for twelve years. Charlie admitted, "I believe Mel Pender, Ronnie Ray Smith, Jim Hines, and myself could have cut that time to 37.0 flat, if I hadn't been hurt."

Charlie's educational credentials include a BA and two MA degrees. He also served over twenty years of active U.S. Army duty before retiring as a major. He's been inducted into the Drake (Relays) Hall of Fame, the USA Track and Field Hall of Fame, the U.S. Olympic Hall of Fame and the 2015 University of Nebraska Hall of Fame.

I first met Charlie in Lincoln when I asked him to do a television public service announcement for the military, since we were both officers. This led to me interviewing him and writing a series of articles for both civilian and military newspapers and magazines. We spent many hours in his Lincoln home telling each other war stories: he about his track career and me about my U.S. Army flying career as a medical evacuation helicopter pilot in Vietnam combat. In all the hours we spent together, the only thing he ever asked of me was to take him on a two-hour helicopter flight around Lincoln and Southeast Nebraska, where we both retired.

In succeeding years, Charlie had to deal with many physical challenges such as a medical diagnosis of uncontrolled diabetes at age forty-eight and heart disease at age fifty-eight. He underwent successful triple-bypass heart surgery in 2002. When he turned sixty, he began experiencing a lack of mobility and had difficulty with balance and walking. Tests revealed compressed disks in his neck. Again, in 2005, he underwent surgery.

At the age of sixty-four, Charlie endured a second neck

surgery for his spinal stenosis condition (a tightening of the spinal column on his spinal cord). That surgery affected the use of his legs and he became unable to walk under his own power. This was a devastating emotional and psychological blow for someone once recognized as the "fastest human on the planet."

It was during these trying moments when Charlie and I had long conversations about spiritual matters. He was at the Madonna Rehabilitation Hospital in Lincoln, after having spent two and a half weeks in intensive care where he almost died at St. Elizabeth Regional Hospital. There, I wasn't interacting with that former brash young sprint champion. This time it was different.

The conversations continued after his release.

"I now believe that faith in God is all you have," Charlie began, "When I went to the chapel at Madonna, there's a peace that comes over you when you're in God's house. You're supposed to tell Him how you feel and stop worrying about it. Just thank Him for what He's given you and let it go."

In 2010, his diabetes required a kidney transplant.

"Before that transplant, when I was doing dialysis," Charlie began, "I'd read the Bible. I found that man often learns the hard way. We all make mistakes. Sometimes we're all hardheaded about dealing with God. Why do some people find out early and some find out late? I'm definitely a late finder.

"What if I believed back then what I believe now?" Charlie continued. "Would I have been a better person?" He answered his own question. "Yeah, because I'd have understood that my life is about God's blessing on me. And I don't think my life back then was about God's blessing on me. I was just there.

"There are two kinds of people," Charlie said, "Givers and

takers. The first part of my life I was a taker. I always wanted stuff. And now I'm giving back. So God is testing me, I guess," Charlie admitted. "There are a lot of people who will not accept any power greater than themselves. God is the answer. In the end, He's the only reason why I exist."

On March 14, 2022, seven days before his seventy-eighth birthday, Charlie Greene sprinted out of this world to meet his Maker. In the words of the Apostle Paul in 2 Timothy 4:7 (NIV), *"I have fought the good fight, I have finished the race, I have kept the faith."*

Charlie has crossed his final finish line. I'm fortunate to have known and been able to call him my friend. But most important of all, in his long race to faith and forgiveness, Charlie has now been able to find and finally meet God in the greatest winner's circle of all.

Locked Out

Janet Faye Mueller

I am usually very careful with my keys. I hate the thought of being locked out of anything . . . especially my car. But that dreaded thing happened one cold winter day.

I left the store with an unusually large cartful of groceries. Seeing my car in the distance and wondering if the groceries would all fit, I popped open the trunk with my remote control. Once at the car, I threw my purse in the front seat and locked the car as usual. That way, while I unloaded the groceries and returned the cart, my purse wouldn't be advertising itself in an unlocked car.

This was my well-oiled system.

All the groceries fit, and I returned my cart to the nearest stall. Then I reached into my coat pocket expecting to find my car keys, but only came up with a used Kleenex.

"Keys, where are my keys?" I moaned while patting myself down. Nothing. I frantically tried opening the car doors, but of course, I had locked them! There sat my purse, all tidy and safe, smirking at me . . . with my keys probably inside.

My mind raced. *Oh, I'll just call my Larry and have him come rescue me.* Again, my hands searched my coat pockets. Nothing! My phone was in my purse, too. Sigh.

I had left the trunk open, which I thought might be my salvation. Was it possible to push the back seats forward from inside the trunk? I saw a young man approaching my area and called out to him. "Young man, do you know if there is a way to gain entrance to this car from the trunk?"

Puzzled, he looked inside and responded, "I don't think so."

He seemed friendly enough so I asked him if I could use his phone to call my husband. He happily obliged.

"Honey, I'm locked out of my car. Are you on your way home from your errands? Can you turn around and rescue me?" I sheepishly asked.

"I don't carry your car key with me. I'll have to go home and get it," he replied.

By now, I was angry at myself for stupidly leaving my keys in my purse and then locking them in the car. I had a long wait ahead of me, and I hate wasting time!

Slamming the trunk down, I marched back into the store to wait the forty-five minutes it would take Larry to get there. The magazines did not hold my interest long, so I went back out to the store lobby to watch and wait.

Suddenly, a thought popped into my mind: "Check your back pocket." I had checked my front coat pockets over and over because that's where I always put my keys. It hadn't occurred to me to check my back jean pockets. My hand quickly flew to the right pocket, and a "Hallelujah!" welled up inside me. Indeed, there were my car keys!

Feeling foolish yet triumphant, I raced back to the car to grab my phone and call my husband. "The keys are found! They were in my back pocket all along!"

On the drive home, I couldn't help but rehearse how that thought, "Check your back pocket," seemingly dropped out of nowhere, because I *never* put anything in my back pockets.

How often the key to solving a problem is right inside you or beside you! As close as your back pocket.

As close as the Holy Spirit.

~ 40 ~

The Wayward Son

Bob Blundell

I first read the parable of The Prodigal Son, from Luke's gospel when in the early stages of my journey toward the Lord. At that point in my life my understanding of God's Word was limited to a literal interpretation of Scripture. I often missed the true essence of the messages Jesus told in the New Testament. I remember finishing the chapter and setting my Bible down on the desk, unnerved by what I had read. The story had struck me square in the face. You see, I was part of the story but not in the way most people would understand.

I was the older son.

Growing up in a small Texas town in the 60s, my younger brother and I were reared as I suspect my father had been brought up. He was a harsh disciplinarian who taught us to respect authority, work hard, and never make excuses for our failures. These rules were strictly enforced, and I did my best to avoid disappointing my parents, my teachers, then later my employers. I worked hard to apply these teachings as I evolved into an adult.

In my mid-thirties, I dove into my career in pursuit of tangible things valued in our world, such as money and status. I desperately sought the admiration and respect of the people around me. With each promotion I received, or possession I acquired, I felt a momentary rush of joy. But like the pleasure we receive from all earthly things, my happiness quickly faded, and I looked to the next challenge, believing status and possessions would help me find true peace.

While I was seeking emotional fulfillment through worldly pleasures, my brother traveled a more volatile road. He stumbled through life, surviving too many self-inflicted wounds to track, squandering every opportunity and gift given to him. With each bad choice he made, a dark cloud of misfortune followed him in his journey. By society's standards he failed in most aspects of his life. However, my parents always stood by him, supported him financially, and defended his actions regardless of the circumstances.

I grew to despise him for his behavior, and harbored resentment toward my parents for not holding him to the same standards we had grown up with. Over his lifetime, they gave to him repeatedly . . . and he always accepted those gifts without a note of gratitude. I had worked diligently to achieve success. My brother, however, never had to earn his way in life. Everything was given to him. Much like the prodigal son.

In Luke chapter 15, Jesus tells a story of a man who had two sons. The youngest son demanded he be given the inheritance he would be due if his father died. The father gave him his share and the son fled the country, spending it foolishly on a life of debauchery and sin. Eventually he returned, penniless and ashamed. But instead of being rebuked and rejected by his father, his father welcomed him home with a celebration.

The oldest son, who had faithfully served his father all his life, was taken aback by his father's generosity toward his brother.

For years I was blind to the true meaning of this powerful story of redemption and relentless love. In the verses, I could only see the flaws of my family as characters in the plot, and the egregious behavior of the younger son, much like my brother's. It took years for my eyes to be opened and the truth to be revealed to me. My gradual enlightenment was purely a result of God's work in my life. But the clarity I saw was not only about the sins of the younger brother. My own journey and transactions became clear to me.

For over forty years, I pursued meaningless objects, material things which could be earned, bought, or possessed. God was neither a part of my life, nor scarcely even a word in my vocabulary.

Twice He called upon me, and twice I denied him.

First, He summoned me, as a teenager, to the front of a small Presbyterian church. I felt a powerful presence urging me to stand and walk toward the pulpit and accept Him in my life, but I was frightened and remained in my seat until the force subsided.

Twenty years later, He beckoned me again, this time through a coworker. I knelt in prayer in a small conference room at work, accepting Christ in my life. Rebirth. I became involved in a church, and my view of what was important in the world began to change. But unfortunately, two years later, the flame in my heart began to flicker and I returned to a life focused on self-indulgence.

I was driven by a need to seek recognition and respect from others, versus paying homage to the One who gave me life. Every thought I had and action I took was focused on myself, whether it was through attainment of financial gain, promotion, or physical pleasure. My pursuit of worldly things eventually took me to a dark place in my life, resulting in divorce and a pressing guilt that threatened to overcome me.

In my blindness and vanity, I had ignored my own transgressions against God. I couldn't see that my sins, though different from my brother's, were no less hurtful to Him.

In short, I was the wayward son.

In a society filled with temptations, most of us are prodigal sons and daughters at various times in our lives. We turn away from Him, seeking fulfillment and joy from worldly things. We revere false idols, whether they are people, possessions, or pleasure. And in our flawed logic we often hesitate to seek Him because we believe our transgressions are unpardonable, unworthy of His love and forgiveness.

But Jesus gave us this parable so we would never lose sight of the message of God's mercy and His infinite love.

In memory, remnants of the resentment I felt about my brother still remain, much like a thorn embedded beneath my skin. But for now, I view him as a person much like me: a sinner who needs God's forgiveness.

I sometimes think of the father in the story, and the great suffering he must have endured when his youngest son demanded his inheritance. That is surely the same pain God endures when we commit sin. Yet despite our failures and flaws, He is always there waiting for the lost to find our way and return — whether we're the younger prodigal or the older wayward son.

~ 41 ~

Enjoying the Journey

Diana Leagh Matthews

When Mama and I take a road trip together it is always an adventure. With our lack of sense of direction, we are guaranteed to get lost and have a ton of laughs.

I'd been researching our family history for years and wanted more information on my grandmother's family. Thankfully, we could drive to Swannanoa, North Carolina within about two hours. We took my grandmother with us to visit the area her paternal grandfather had moved his family from after generations of living in the area.

Upon reaching Swannanoa, we easily found the cemeteries we were seeking and walked through them, taking pictures. But I still had a few questions, so we went in search of the local library. I wasn't sure what it might have but I was eager to find out.

We drove around looking for the library but couldn't find it. Stopping, we asked a man for directions, but again its location evaded us.

We stopped a second time and asked directions, but it continued to evaded us.

Laughing as we drove around in circles searching for the elusive location, we began to wonder if the library even existed.

Finally, we stopped at a fast food restaurant and while there asked for directions. The woman we asked was full of information and history of the area and we had a wonderful conversation. Following her directions, we found the library . . . and discovered we had been a block off the entire time.

While the library didn't have what we needed, the journey is one we still fondly remember more than two decades later.

Often in life, we search for answers to a dilemma. We set our eyes on our destination, and because of that we can feel lost at times. But, the Lord's heart is set on the journey. Only once we're on the other side do we see the twists and turns along the way. Within these twists and turns are lessons, chance encounters, and laughter we would have missed otherwise.

King David wrote, *"I wait for the L*ORD*, my soul does wait, And in His word do I hope"* (Psalm 130:5 NASB).

While you wait for the Lord, are you enjoying the journey?

About the Authors

Ellen Andersen is a freelance writer living in Mauldin, South Carolina. She has contributed to www.christiandevotions.us, and has had short stories published in *Buckets of Hope*, *Loving Moments* and *Cool-inary Moments*.

Ellen is a Stephen Minister in her church, where she uses her gift of encouragement to help others going through a myriad of difficult circumstances. She enjoys gardening, baking, and going to the theater.

Bob Blundell is a former mid-level manager who spent his career in the oil industry. Since returning from a pilgramage to Israel in 2018, he has written over 100 works in both Christian as well as secular magazines and journals and is a winner of the 2021 Christian Writers Award. He has had numerous stories published in other *Divine Moments* books. His first solo book, *Crossroads - A Journey from Communist China to Christ*, was released in February 2024.

Sheryl H. Boldt has loved writing ever since she saw her mother, an aspiring author, pecking on her Royal manual typewriter. That inspiration has led Sheryl to write fiction and non-fiction for children and adults. Her articles have been published in magazines such as *War Cry* and *The Upper Room*. Sheryl's weekly column appears in at least 31 newspapers across the South and her award-winning story, "Grandma's Little Helpers," delights small and not-so-small readers alike.

Because of her past battles with anorexia/bulimia and depression, Sheryl looks for fresh ways to connect struggling people to God's Word. A strong believer in accountability, Sheryl mentors ladies via email, social media, and accountability groups. Read her devotions on her blog, TodayCanBeDifferent.net.

Leigh-Anne Burley is published in nonfiction, fiction, and poetry. Some of her 35 published stories include: "A Family Within a Universe" in *Ariel Chart International Literary Journal,* "Unpredictable Weather Patterns" on *Little Blue Marble,* "Mr. Mouse and Mr. Clarkes Unite in The Universe" in *Spaceports and Spidersilk,* "The Thread" in *Deccomp Journal,* "Home Plate Slide" in *The Dribble Drabble Review,* and "Threshold Crossings" in *Toasted Cheese Literary Journal.*

Leigh-Anne enjoys walking, reading, writing, knitting, and movies. She and her husband of 43 years live in Virginia. They have three children and six grandchildren.

Theresa Cates is a resident of Birmingham, Alabama. She and her husband of 50 years have four adult children and seventeen grandchildren. Writing stories for her grandchildren and others to enjoy is one way she seeks to capture special memories with them.

A Sunday School teacher for many years, she has a deep love of Scripture and a desire to encourage others in their spiritual walk.

An avid quilter, Theresa enjoys teaching and sharing her love of quilting through a local ministry to victims of human trafficking.

Lola Di Giulio De Maci is a retired teacher whose stories have appeared in numerous editions of *Chicken Soup for the Soul, Divine Moments, Guideposts, Reminisce, Los Angeles Times,* and various children's publications and newspaper columns. Lola has a Master of Arts in Education and English, and a Doctorate in Education. She writes overlooking California's San Bernardino Mountains.

Diana C. Derringer, author of *Beyond Bethlehem and Calvary: 12 Dramas for Christmas, Easter, and More!* shares hope and joy through more than 1,200 devotions, articles, dramas, Bible studies, planning guides, and poems in 70-plus publications and anthologies. She also writes radio dramas and *Questions About Life* television programs for Christ to the World Ministries, and shares weekly blog posts on *Words, Wit, and Wisdom: Life Lessons from English Expressions.*

Diana speaks at churches, schools, and community events and has taught workshops for the Kentucky Christian Writers Conference. Her adventures as a social worker, adjunct professor, youth Bible study teacher, friendship family for international university students, and caregiver for her husband supply a constant flow of writing ideas. Connect with Diana at dianaderringer.com or on Facebook, Twitter, LinkedIn, Instagram, Goodreads, Pinterest, and her Amazon page.

Tanja Dufrene's purpose in writing is to stimulate readers to wholesome thinking (2 Peter 3:1). While leading a ladies group, she recognized the sincerity of many Christ followers, but was concerned about their lack of biblical knowledge. So, she began writing weekly devotional emails, hoping to inspire her readers to draw closer to God. Some of those writing are found in *Artesian Zeal*, her first devotional book. Another ladies' Bible study resulted in the *Warrior of the Word* series. Both are available through Amazon and Barnes & Noble. She shares a daily minute devotional on her *Warrior of the Word* Facebook page. Tanja became an ordained minister in 2011. You can follow her on LinkedIn, Twitter, Instagram, Pinterest, and her website www.WarrioroftheWord. faith, or contact her via email at WarrioroftheWord@yahoo.com.

Terri Elders, a licensed clinical social worker and lifelong writer and editor, has contributed to nearly 150 anthologies, including multiple editions of *Chicken Soup for the Soul.* She writes feature articles and travel pieces for regional, national, and international publications. Terri lives in her native southern California, not far from her beloved Pacific Ocean. You can friend her on Facebook.

Carol Graham is a charismatic master storyteller whose message is passionate and uplifting. With riveting true stories, Carol conveys how to overcome doubt, fear, trauma, and everything in between. She is an expert in surviving against all odds.

Carol received the *Woman of Impact Award* and *Author of the Year* for her memoir, *Battered Hope,* and the global award for *One Woman – Fearless* given to women who have faced their fears and made the world a better place for women to thrive.

The award-winning author is also a keynote speaker, prayer coach, teacher, podcaster, YouTuber, and dog rescuer.

Lydia E. Harris has been married to her college sweetheart, Milt, for more than 50 years. She enjoys spending time with her family, which includes two married children and five grandchildren. She is the author of three books for grandparents: *Preparing My Heart for Grandparenting: for Grandparents at Any Stage of the Journey, In the Kitchen with Grandma: Stirring Up Tasty Memories Together,* and the newly released *GRAND Moments: Devotions Inspired by Grandkids.*

With a master's degree in Home Economics, Lydia creates and tests recipes with her grandchildren for Focus on the Family children's magazines. She also pens the column "A Cup of Tea with Lydia," which is published in the US and Canada. It's no wonder she is known as "Grandma Tea."

Tom Hooker, a native of Mississippi, and his family have lived in Hendersonville, North Carolina since 1988. Tom has had short stories and poems published in a number of literary journals across the nation. Poetry credits include *Yourdailypoem.com, Creative Inspirations*, and *Teach.Write.* He and Gary Ader co-authored a novel titled *The War Never Ends*. He wrote *Twenty-five Angels*, as a solo novel. His newest novel, now available, is titled *Year of the White Dog*. Tom has served as facilitator of the Blue Ridge Writers Group in Hendersonville since 2007.

Helen L. Hoover and her husband of 60 years are retired and live in the Ozark Mountains of south-central Missouri. Sewing, reading, knitting, tending the flower and veggie gardens, and helping her husband with home repair occupy her time now. Word Aflame Publishing, *The Secret Place*, Word Action Publication, *The Quiet Hour*, *The Lutheran Digest*, Light and Life Communications, *Chicken Soup for the Soul*, and Victory in Grace have published her devotionals and personal articles. Visits with their two living children, and their grandchildren and great-grandchildren are treasured.

Alice Klies, president of Northern Arizona Word Weavers, a chapter of Word Weavers International, has had nonfiction and fiction stories published in 25 anthologies. She is a 16-time contributor to *Chicken Soup for the Soul* books and has had articles published in *Angels on Earth*, *AARP* and *Wordsmith Journal*. She has also been featured in the *Women of Distinction* magazine. Her novel, *Pebbles in My Way*, fiction based on her testimony, was released in 2017 and *Chased by the Hound of Heaven* was released in 2021.

Alice serves on two non-profit boards: The Verde Valley Humane Society and Sisterhood Connections Foundation LTD. A retired teacher, who resides with her husband in beautiful Cottonwood, Arizona, she prays her stories cause readers to smile, laugh or even cry good tears.

Diana Leagh Matthews is a vocalist, speaker, writer, life coach, and genealogist who has a heart for sharing God's love. During the day, she is a certified Activities Director for a skilled nursing facility.

A Christian Communicators graduate, she has been published on a variety of websites and in anthologies,including the *Divine Moments* books. She is the author of *90 Breath Prayers for the Healthcare Professional, 90 Breath Prayers for the Caregiver, the 90 Breath Prayer Journal,* and *90 Breath Prayers for those with Health Challenges.* Diana currently resides in South Carolina. Whether writing, singing, researching history, or working with seniors in nursing homes, she longs to shine for Christ. Visit her at www.DianaLeighMatthews.com and www.alookthrutime.com.

Carol Ogle McCracken has been a Bible teacher for 20 years, serving on church staff and in women's ministry. She currently serves as the Minister of Discipleship at her home church where she teaches a weekly Wednesday night women's Bible study. Carol hosts the *Your Daily Bible Verse* podcast and does a Daily Inspiration on Christian Mix 106 web radio. But her greatest passion is to make the Bible come alive for women, connecting scripture to a real relationship with Jesus. Her book *Wisdom, Where to Find It if You've Lost, Forgotten, or Never Had It* is available on Amazon. Find her at www.CarolMcCracken.com.

Beverly Hill McKinney has published over 700 inspirational articles in such publications as *Good Old Days, Sharing, Breakthrough Intercessor, Just Between Us, Woman Alive, P31* and *Plus Magazine.* She has devotions in *Cup of Comfort Devotional: Daily Reflections of God's Love and Grace, Open Windows, God Still Meets Needs* and *God Still Leads and Guides.* Her stories have been featured in anthologies such as *Christmas Miracles, Men of Honor,* Guidepost's *Extraordinary Answers to Prayer, Christian Miracles, Precious Precocious Moments, Additional Christmas Moments* and *Loving Moments.* She has also self-published *Through the Parsonage Window* and *Whispers from God: Poems of Inspiration.* Beverly, who lives in Oregon, graduated from the Jerry B. Jenkins Christian Writer's Guild at both Apprentice and Journeyman levels.

Norma C. Mezoe has been a published writer for 38 years. Her writing has appeared in books, devotionals, Sunday school take-home papers, magazines, and online. She became a Christian at the age of 15, but didn't grow spiritually in a significant way until a crisis, at the age of 33, brought her into a closer relationship with the Lord. Her desire is to honor God with her writing, and to encourage and point others to Jesus Christ. Norma may be contacted at: normacm@tds.net.

Lynn Mosher has had her socked feet firmly planted in the Midwest since she drew her first breath. She was saved at the renowned Billy Graham crusade in New York City in 1957. Although an upheaval of illness has stalked her for many years, her deepest passion (alongside cooking/baking and crafting) is sharing her devotionals and inspirational stories through her website, other websites, and in published anthologies, and her graphics on social media, fulfilling God's call on her life to encourage others and glorify the Lord with her writing. She writes a weekly devotional called *Letters from the Couch*, which can be subscribed to at: http://eepurl.com/b5n-Pf.

Vicki H. Moss is former Editor-at-Large and Contributing Editor for *Southern Writers Magazine* where she interviewed authors and contributed articles on writing in addition to blogging for the magazine's *Suite T* blog. She also wrote a weekly column as a pundit for the *American Daily Herald*. As a workshop instructor for writers conferences, Vicki teaches from her books *How to Write for Kids' Magazines* and *Writing with Voice*. With over 750 articles published, she co-authored the book *Nailed It!* and contributed to Cecil Murphey's book, *I Believe in Heaven*. When Vicki's not gardening, making author visits, or teaching a class on "Writing the Stories Behind the Recipes," she writes poetry that's published in magazines and her books on writing.

Janet Faye Mueller writes from a small, rural community in northeast Indiana. She has a penchant for drawing spiritual analogies from everyday observations. Devotionals, short stories, "God stories," and poetry provide the perfect outlet for these analogies. Janet founded Heartland Writers Circle, a church-based ministry of creative writers. She is also a Creative Writing Leader and Administrative Assistant for United Adoration, a nonprofit organization whose mission is to revitalize the creativity of the local church. Janet writes a blog, *Views From the Empty Nest*, and has been published in a variety of magazines. She and her husband are celebrating 40 years of marriage this year. They have two adult sons, a beautiful daughter-in-law, and two adorable grandsons. Janet enjoys woman-talk, good coffee, encouraging encounters, and hearty laughter!

Robert B. Robeson has had 940 articles, short stories and poems published in 73 anthologies and 330 publications in 130 countries. This includes *Reader's Digest, Writer's Digest, Positive Living, Vietnam Combat, Official Karate, Soldier of Fortune* and *Writer's Yearbook 2014*, among others. After retiring as a lieutenant colonel from a 27½-year Army career as a helicopter medical evacuation pilot, he served as a newspaper managing editor and columnist. He has a BA from the University of Maryland, College Park and has completed extensive undergraduate and graduate work in journalism at the University of Nebraska, Lincoln. He lives in Lincoln, Nebraska with Phyllis, his wife of 54 years.

Sue Schlesman is an author, teacher, podcaster, and church leader. With a Masters in Theology and Culture, she is active in teaching and writing about transformative faith. Her book *Soulspeak: Praying Change into Unexpected Places* won a Selah Award in 2020. She has co-written a children's Bible, which releases in 2024. Sue writes for Salem Web Network radio and

Crosswalk.com on topics of faith, church, and relationships. Sue and her husband, Shane, are passionate about creating diverse, compassionate faith communities and mentoring healthy church leaders. Their podcast, *Stress Test,* focuses on managing leadership health and tension. Sue loves traveling and hanging out with Shane, their three sons, and their two daughters-in-law. Sue and Shane have been married for 34 years.

Susan Schwartz has been an avid writer for over 25 years, doing everything from writing freelance articles to editing manuscripts for other authors. She loves writing horror stories that will twist you in knots by the end. Her alter ego is an Operating Room Nurse/Nurse Educator who creates tales from the interesting and weird things she has seen. She is a member of the Horror Writers Association and the Virginia Writers Club where she served as President of the Richmond Chapter and 1st Vice-President of the state organization. She has two novels in the works, a paranormal romance and a medical thriller. Her paranormal book, *Haunted Inns and Hotels in Virginia,* released in 2023. Visit her website at susanschwartzauthor.com.

Christina Sinisi, a member of American Christian Fiction Writers, writes stories about families, both the broken and blessed. Her works include a semi-finalist in the Amazon Breakthrough Novel Award contest and the American Title IV Contest where she appeared in the top ten in *Romantic Times* magazine. By day, she is a psychology professor and lives in the Low Country of South Carolina with her husband, two children, and her crazy cat, Chessie Mae. Visit her at Christina Sinisi-Author on Facebook and christinasinisi.com.

Laura Sweeney facilitates Writers for Life in Iowa and Illinois. She represented the Iowa Arts Council at the First International Teaching Artist's Conference in Oslo, Norway. Her poems and prose appear in more than 60 journals and 10 anthologies in the US, Canada, Britain, Indonesia, and China. Her recent awards include a scholarship to the Sewanee Writer's Conference. In 2021, she received an Editor's Prize in Flash Discourse from *Open: Journal of Arts & Letters,* and the Poetry Society of Michigan's Barbara Sykes Memorial Humor Award. Two of her poems appear in the anthology *Impact: Personal Portraits of Activism,* which received an American Book Fest Best Book Award in its Current Events category and finalist in the Social Change category. She is a PhD candidate in English/Creative Writing, at Illinois State University.

Annmarie B. Tait resides in Harleysville, Pennsylvania with her husband, Joe Beck, where they are at last embarking on retirement. In addition to writing tales about growing up in her large, Irish-Catholic family and the memories they made, she also cultivates her passion for, cooking, crocheting, Scrabble and as of late, "Wordle." She also enjoys singing and recording Irish and American Folk Songs. Annmarie's stories have been published in several volumes of *Patchwork Path, Chicken Soup for the Soul,* the HCI *Ultimate* series, *Reminisce* magazine, and the Blue Mountain Press publication *Irish Inspirations.* Contact Annmarie at: irishbloom@aol.com.

Ann Tatlock is a novelist, children's book author, freelance editor, and writing mentor. After earning a master's degree in journalism from Wheaton College, she began her career as a writer and editor for Billy Graham's *Decision* magazine. She makes her home in North Carolina, where she spends her happiest moments taking care of her granddaughter, Ellie.

Cecil Taylor, founder of Cecil Taylor Ministries, is dedicated to teaching Christians how to live a 7-day practical faith. He is the author of two award-winning books, *The Next Thing: A Christian*

Model for Dealing with Crisis in Personal Life and *Live Like You're Loved: Living in the Freedom and Immediacy of God's Love*. Small-group video lessons and study guides accompany each book.

With more than 30 years' experience as an adult Sunday school teacher and as many years in youth ministry, Cecil has impacted lives in local churches throughout his adult life. He founded Cecil Taylor Ministries to broaden that impact through books, video studies, articles, blogging, podcasting, and speaking engagements. Visit his website: https://www.CecilTaylorMinistries.com or contact him at Cecil@CecilTaylorMinistries.com.

Laura Taylor's adventures have taken her throughout Europe, the Philippines, and the Eastern seaboard. She and her husband, Terry, currently reside in rural South Carolina.

A prodigal daughter rescued by the King of kings, Laura strives to live in the moments and momentum of God's amazing grace.

After 12 years of teaching, Laura felt called to pursue her writing career full-time. She is a 3rd degree black belt, martial arts instructor, author, and proud mom of 4 incredible sons and a wayward pup named Harley.

Laura earned an M.Ed. in TESOL (teaching English to speakers of other languages) from Southeastern University. She is the author of the children's book *EE Otter and the Bullfrog Bullies*.

Her work has been published through *christiandevotions.us* and *Living Real Magazine*.